D1311598

Have You Ever Seen a Hearse Pulling a Trailer?

Have You Ever Seen a Hearse Pulling a Trailer?

James W. Moore

Abingdon Press
NASHVILLE

HAVE YOU EVER SEEN A HEARSE PULLING A TRAILER?

Copyright © 2009 by Abingdon Press

All rights reserved.

No part of this work may be reproduced or transmitted in any form or by any means, electronic or mechanical, including photocopying and recording, or by any information storage or retrieval system, except as may be expressly permitted by the 1976 Copyright Act or in writing from the publisher. Requests for permission can be addressed to Abingdon Press, P.O. Box 801, 201 Eighth Avenue South, Nashville, TN 37202-0801, or e-mailed to permissions@abingdonpress.com.

This book is printed on acid-free paper.

Library of Congress Cataloging-in-Publication Data

Moore, James W. (James Wendell), 1938-
  Have you ever seen a hearse pulling a trailer? / James W. Moore.
    p. cm.
  ISBN 978-0-687-46484-5 (pbk. : alk. paper)
  1. Christian life. 2. Values. 3. Conduct of life. I. Title.
  BV4501.3.M6625 2009
  248.4—dc22

                                                                    2009015462

All scripture quotations unless noted otherwise are taken from the New Revised Standard Version of the Bible, copyright 1989, Division of Christian Education of the National Council of the Churches of Christ in the United States of America. Used by permission. All rights reserved.

Scripture quotations marked RSV are taken from the Revised Standard Version of the Bible, copyright 1952 [2nd edition, 1971] by the Division of Christian Education of the National Council of the Churches of Christ in the United States of America. Used by permission. All rights reserved.

Scripture quotations marked KJV are taken from the King James or Authorized Version of the Bible.

Scripture quotations marked ESV are taken from The Holy Bible, English Standard Version®, copyright © 2001 by Crossway Bibles, a publishing ministry of Good News Publishers. Used by permission. All rights reserved.

09 10 11 12 13 14 15 16 17 18 — 10 9 8 7 6 5 4 3 2
MANUFACTURED IN THE UNITED STATES OF AMERICA

In memory of our beloved family members and dear friends who lived out their days on this earth with love for God and love for others, and who inspired us by the way they "set [their] minds on things that are above" (Colossians 3:2).

CONTENTS

INTRODUCTION

You Can't Take It with You

All of our lives we have heard the saying "You can't take it with you!" That good advice has been drilled into our brains repeatedly by our parents, our grandparents, our pastors, our teachers, and our friends. And yet, our materialistic world teaches the opposite in the most creative and persuasive Madison Avenue ways. Television commercials, radio advertisements, newspaper ads, and Internet solicitations bombard us constantly and repeatedly with overt and subliminal messages that try (often with great success) to entice us to believe that there are certain "things" that we definitely must have in our possession if we are going to be happy, satisfied, and successful.

The right car, the right clothes, the right cologne, the right cosmetics, the right house in the right neighborhood, the right "toys," the right food and drink, the right gadgets—these are the things that will bring happiness and fulfillment, our modern-day world tells us with loud shouts and enticing whispers. And nothing could be further from the truth! The Scriptures tell us not to be duped or taken in by these false claims. The Scriptures tell us to set our affections "on things that are above." And the Scriptures remind us that material things are not the answer because they are not eternal. They are not of God. They don't last. They don't fulfill really. They will rust and corrode and go out of style. They will never satisfy for long.

It is nice to have money and the things that money can buy, but every now and then we need to stop and check to see if we have the things that money can't buy—things like love, gratitude, hope, faith, generosity, commitment, serenity, and a sense of purpose and meaning. A good relationship with God and good relationships with others, these are the real riches of life.

We see this vividly in the story of the rich young ruler. He had it all: youth, wealth, and power—"the big three" that Madison Avenue advertisers love so much and tell us boldly that we must have. Youth, wealth, and power—the rich young ruler had all of these. He was a *rich young ruler* and yet he was unfulfilled, not satisfied, not happy. Despite having all that he possessed, there was an emptiness, a hunger for something more. He knew it; he felt it. There was a hole in his soul. Those material things that he possessed in spades did not satisfy him. Something was missing. Give him credit. He did realize that the answer was with Jesus Christ; but, sadly, he could not walk away from his old life and consequently he could not make the "leap of faith." So as far as we know, he missed out on the new life with Christ. Over the years we have used this story to underscore the cost of discipleship, but in a real sense the story is about the riches in discipleship. Jesus is showing us here through this story that discipleship is better than dollars; it is wealth beyond counting.

So, the message is clear: you can't take it with you, so

give your life and energy not to things that fade and rust and corrode and go out of style, but rather to the values and commitments and relationships that transcend the "things of this world," to the values and commitments and relationships that are eternal because they are of God. Or as a bumper sticker I recently saw so creatively put it, "Have you ever seen a hearse pulling a trailer?"

CHAPTER ONE

You Can't Take It with You, So Live Confidently Now

"Have You Ever Seen a Hearse Pulling a Trailer?"

SCRIPTURE: 2 TIMOTHY 1:3-7

O ur grandson Paul is twelve years old now. For the first years of his life, he was pretty content to let his older sister, Sarah, do the talking, and that worked very well because she talked enough for both of them—and then some. But then when Paul was three and a half, Sarah went to first grade and was away from home much more because of her school schedule. Paul exploded verbally, and soon he was talking our ears off too.

He called to tell us about his first full day at school. He said the teachers had given each one of the three-year-olds a basket (at an earlier session) and had asked them to fill the basket up with some of their favorite things and then bring the basket back to school to "show and tell" why they loved these favorite things so much. We asked Paul what he had put in his basket. He answered in intricate detail: his stuffed bear; his toy train engine; one of his fish pillows; a plastic dinosaur; a football; and, most important of all, a piece of his "blankie."

We then asked Paul about what was his favorite thing at school and he said, "At recess, I kissed a girl."

"You kissed a girl at recess?" we asked.

"Yep."

"Well, did she like that?"

Paul said, and I quote him precisely, "Oh, yeah!"

Now, that is the picture of confidence, and it is pretty cute in a little three-and-a-half-year-old boy, especially if that little three-and-a half-year-old happens to be your grandson. But it raises an interesting and crucial question that I want to place before us now, namely this: Where do you put your confidence? In whom or in what do you put your confidence? What is it that makes you feel good and confident about life? What makes you feel safe and secure? What gives you hope for tomorrow? What enables you to sleep well at night?

The world is pretty tricky and sometimes downright deceptive about this. The world tells us to put our confidence in money, in possessions, in belongings, in success, in pills, in liquor, in clout, in securities. (Look at that—we even call them "securities.") In a nutshell, the world tells us dramatically and repeatedly in the most creative and persuasive Madison Avenue ways to put our confidence in material things. But then, I saw that bumper sticker the other day that had these words: "Have you ever seen a hearse pulling a trailer?"

Now, what was that all about? Well, that bumper sticker was simply saying in a modern-day way what the old-timers have been saying for years: "You can't take it with you when you go!" You can't take the earthly things you've accumulated with you when you die, so you had better not put your trust and confidence in material things. There are some things in life money can't buy. In fact, the *best* things in life money can't buy.

This truth was brought home powerfully to me some years ago. The son of a very wealthy man smashed his sports car into a tree. I went to the emergency room to try to help the family. The boy's father was a nice guy but his major motive in life had been making money. He was running up and down the halls of the hospital waving hundred-dollar bills in his hand, trying to give them to the doctors and nurses, and saying, "Here, take this. You've got to get in there and save my boy's life. Here's a hundred-dollar bill. Save my boy. Take this, I'm counting on you."

The doctors and nurses would not take the money. They would only say, "We are doing everything we can." But it was too late; the boy didn't make it. His father ran and fell into my arms like a little lost child and cried his eyes out, sobbing so hard his shoulders were shaking. Finally, he pulled back. He took all that money—all those hundred-dollar bills—and threw them on the floor, and through his sobs he said, "Jim, all these years I have put my trust and confidence in all the wrong things. I have money to burn and now, in this moment, it is not worth anything. Where do I find the resources to stand this?"

Let me ask you something. Have you ever felt like that? Have you ever had an experience like that? So agonizing, so heartbreaking, so gut-wrenching that you cried out, "Where do I find the resources to stand this?" Now, the answer to that painful question is found in our key scripture for this chapter. This is precisely what the

Apostle Paul is talking about here. The words of 2 Timothy encourage us to be strong in the Lord, to stand firm in the faith, and to put our confidence in God. The early church was facing many difficulties, formidable threats, cruel persecutions, confusing heresies, and hurtful losses. It would have been so easy for those early Christians to get discouraged, perplexed, scared, and disillusioned.

The task before them was so huge. The enemies were so real. So, in 2 Timothy, we find these helpful words of encouragement, powerful words of scripture, which over the years many Christians have committed to memory to help them stand tall when the going is rough. Words such as these:

> *I know whom I have believed, and I am sure that he is able to guard until that Day what has been entrusted to me. (2 Timothy 1:12 RSV)*

> *I have fought the good fight, I have finished the race, I have kept the faith. Henceforth there is laid up for me the crown of righteousness. (2 Timothy 4:7-8 RSV)*

And then, here, too, we of course find our text for this chapter:

> *Rekindle the gift of God that is within you . . . ; for God did not give us a spirit of cowardice, but rather a spirit of power and of love. (2 Timothy 1:6-7)*

Those are strong words of encouragement reminding us that because of the power of God, the grace of God, and the watchcare of God, we can be confident!

Now, to bring this closer to home, let me give you three thoughts to try on for size, thoughts that emerge out of Paul's words in 2 Timothy.

First of All, We Can Put Our Confidence in the Promise of God

Some years ago, a brilliant and yet eccentric mathematics professor assigned to his students an incredibly difficult math problem for homework. The next day he asked some of the students to go to the board and write out their solutions to the intricate problem. One student after another went to the blackboard, and when they finished their computations the professor simply stated, "No, I'm sorry. That's wrong. Please be seated."

Finally, one student was left. He had worked all night on this math problem. He walked up and wrote his answer on the board. The professor once again said, "That's wrong! Someone else put that answer up there earlier. Didn't you hear me say before that it was wrong?"

"Yes, sir, I did," replied the student, "but it's not wrong. This is the correct answer."

But the professor fired back at him, "That is *not* the correct answer. I'm sorry. You are wrong. Take your seat."

And the student said, "Sir, I'll be happy to be seated. But with all due respect, I must tell you that you are wrong. This is the correct answer."

The professor looked at him intently and asked, "Are you sure?"

"Yes, sir," answered the student. "I am absolutely sure."

Then the professor smiled and said, "Well, you are right. It is the correct answer!" Then the professor turned to the others in the class and said, "People are looking for solutions today. And they want to be sure that those who provide the solutions have total confidence in them. This young man demonstrated today not only that he knows, but also that he *knows* that he knows!"

That's the kind of confidence we need as Christians these days, isn't it? And we can have it because of God's greatest promise. That great promise is underscored over and over in the Bible—the promise that God will never desert us. He will always be there for us. So, we can do our best and trust God for the rest.

The great Old Testament scholar Martin Buber said something toward the end of his life that touched me greatly. He was commenting on that wonderful scene in the book of Exodus when Moses asked God, "What is your name?" And God answered, "I AM WHO I AM." After studying the Hebrew text for many years, Martin Buber said he came to the conclusion that we have mistranslated that verse. Instead of being translated "I AM WHO I AM," Buber said he believed it should read "I SHALL BE THERE." Isn't that beautiful? The name of God is "I SHALL BE THERE"!

When we face the pharaohs of life, the name of God is "I SHALL BE THERE." When we are frightened or lonely or depressed or heartsick, the name of God is "I SHALL BE THERE." When we face sickness or sadness or even death, the name of God is "I SHALL BE THERE." And *that* is where we put our confidence first of all, in this great promise of God to always be there for us.

Second, We Can Put Our Confidence in the Truth of Christ

Some years ago, there was a great professor at Centenary College named Dean R. E. Smith. Dean Smith was a saintly man, a brilliant scholar, an outstanding communicator, and a real friend to the students. He was a legend in his own time. In one of his most famous lectures, Smith would talk to the students about how we discover truth, how we determine what is genuine and what is false. After some discussion, he would suddenly ask the students this question: "How wide is my desk?" The students would look at the desk and then make their best guesses. A variety of answers would ring out.

"I think it's about seventy-two inches wide."

"No, I believe it's more like sixty-eight inches wide."

"Looks like seventy-five to me."

"I'm going to guess seventy-four."

Then some wise guy from the back of the room would say, "Seventy-one and five-sixteenths," and everybody would laugh.

Then Smith would say, "Those are all pretty good guesses, but one of them is more nearly true than the others. Now, how do we determine which one is more accurate? How do we decide which answer is most nearly right and true?" There would be silence in the classroom for a moment and then tentatively someone would suggest, "Get a measuring stick?" "That's right," Smith would say, "To determine which answer is closest to the truth, we have to get a measuring stick and measure." Then Smith would go to the blackboard. He would take a piece of chalk and in silence he would draw the outline of a cross. With that piece of chalk, he would trace over and over the sign of the cross, letting it dramatically sink into the hearts and minds of those students. Then he would stand back and point to that cross and say, "There's your measuring stick! There's your measuring stick for truth!"

Now, look with me at that cross. There's our compass. There's our guiding light. There's our measuring stick for truth. We can put our confidence in that. If the world tries to tell you that it's OK to take advantage of others for your own personal gain; if the world tries to tell you that it's not so bad to lie, cheat, hurt, hold a grudge, or hate; you remember the cross. Remember the truth of Christ.

In recent years, everywhere we would go we'd see young people wearing necklaces with the letters WWJD. Those letters stand for "What Would Jesus Do?" People wearing these letters are trying to remember to measure their actions and their decisions by the truth of Christ. What would Jesus do?

The measuring stick of Christ tells us to be committed to God and compassionate toward others; to be loving and caring and kind; to be just and honest and truthful; to be loyal and merciful and gracious. Anything that doesn't measure up to that is wrong and sinful! So, we can put our confidence in the promise of God to always be with us and in the truth of Christ to always guide us.

Third and Finally, We Can Put Our Confidence in the Strength of the Holy Spirit

Do you remember that scene from *The Sound of Music* where Maria is being sent out from the abbey to be the governess for Captain von Trapp's seven children? She's a little nervous as she walks down the road, but to rally her courage she begins to sing "I Have Confidence": "I have confidence they'll put me to the test. / But I'll make them see I have confidence in me."

When she arrives, however, and sees the huge, elegant, vast von Trapp estate, Maria becomes intimidated for a moment. She stops singing, looks up toward heaven, and says prayerfully to God: "Oh, help."

We can all relate to that, can't we? Sometimes life's problems overwhelm us and all we can do is say prayerfully, "O God, help me!" The good news is that we *can* always count on the Holy Spirit to be there for us and to give us the strength we need.

Dietrich Bonhoeffer put it like this: "God will give us all the strength we need to help us . . . in all time of distress. But [God] never gives it to us in advance, lest we should rely on ourselves and not on [God] alone" (Dietrich Bonhoeffer, *Letters and Papers from Prison* [New York: Simon & Schuster, 1997], 11).

The Apostle Paul said it a long time ago, but it is still so true today: Where do we put our confidence? We put our confidence in the promise of God to always be there for us, in the truth of Christ to always guide us, and in the strength of the Holy Spirit to always uphold us.

CHAPTER TWO

You Can't Take It with You, So Live Faithfully Now

A Faith for Ordinary Times

SCRIPTURE: HEBREWS 10:32-39

Some years ago, when Dr. Harry Emerson Fosdick was pastor of Riverside Church in New York City, he wrote a book entitled *Faith for Tough Times*. It is a classic because it addresses important concerns that rise up within us all: How do we keep our faith when problems come or when tragedy strikes? How do we keep our faith in a hotbed of opposition or when the price is so painful? How do we keep our faith when times are truly tough?

These concerns are very important, but there is another side of the coin that also deserves our attention, namely, how do we keep our faith when times *aren't* so tough? What happens to commitment in the give-and-take of everyday living? How do we hold on to faith in the "daily-ness" of life when times are just ordinary? The author of the book of Hebrews again and again turns our attention to this theme: How do we sustain a vibrant faith when the times are casual or just ordinary?

Over the years in working with people, I have noticed something fascinating, namely, how well people handle the major emergencies of life; how well people rise to the occasion and stand tall against adversity; how well people respond with courage and strength when dramatic or tragic or traumatic things happen to them. You see, it is not the big problems of life that undo us. It's the little things, the daily things, the tiny annoyances, the routine irritations that eat us up and tear us down. We handle the big battles pretty well, only to be ripped apart by little day-to-day frustrations.

We are all familiar with the old and much-used slogan "When the going gets tough, the tough get going." But the corollary to that, which we are so prone to overlook, would be, "When the going is easy, even the tough slack off!" When things are only ordinary, we tend to relax; when the demands are not dramatically challenging, the response is to let down, to overlook, to neglect, to coast, and to fail in ways we often would not do when the pressure is on.

We see this in the world of sports. Sometimes a team will point toward a certain big game and get "up" for that game and play at peak performance against an outstanding opponent and win, only to have a letdown the next week and lose to a mediocre team. When the pressure is on, when the challenge is great, we stand firm only to fall flat when things get back to normal.

Here is the warning the writer of Hebrews lays before us: beware when things are just ordinary; beware when no one wants to crucify you; beware when no hard problem confronts you; beware when no fearsome threat hangs over your head; beware when you drift unchallenged into the ruts of the routine. Your faith may be in no greater danger than in times like these. These are the times, says the writer of Hebrews, when we have to pay attention lest we drift away. It is not when the battle lines are drawn or when the trumpets blare or when the drums roll that most of us either find or lose our faith. Rather, it is when the bills are being paid, when we are caught in traffic, when the shopping is being done, or when the church pledge card is being signed. It is in how we speak to our neighbor, how we relate to our children, how we treat the food server, and how we respond to our coworkers. It is in daily living, routine living, ordinary living that our faith is really affirmed and expressed or else it slips away so silently, so quietly, so gradually that it is gone before we even realize it. Then one day we are jolted to see that our values have become those of the crowd and not of the Christ; our choices have become those of chance and not of commitment; our faith has become convenience instead of obedience; our morality has become custom instead of character.

The truth is that for most of us the real challenge of Christian life and faith is precisely here—in ordinary times, in ordinary places, in the give-and-take of day-to-day living. What advice is there for us? How do we have and hold on to a vibrant and exciting faith when the times aren't so tough and when the days are regular or casual or mundane or ordinary?

The writer of Hebrews is helpful here. He suggests three things: first, the original challenge of discipleship; second, the ongoing commitments of discipleship; and third, the ever-present cost of discipleship.

Let's take a look at these together.

First of All, Remember the Original Challenge of Discipleship

Remember what first challenged you. "Recall those earlier days," he says. Remember how it once was. Remember what inspired you originally. Recall what caused you to make your initial leap of faith. Remember how God first touched you. We could all use that advice from time to time.

I read the other day about a mother who went upstairs into her son's bedroom to wake him, and she said to him, "Get up and get ready. It's almost time to go to church." The son pulled the covers up over his shoulders and turned away from her, saying, "I don't want to go today."

His mother said, "Come on, Son, we always go to church."

He answered, "I'm tired."

"You can rest some other time, we need to go to church this morning," she countered.

Then he said, "I want to sleep in. Sunday morning is the only time I have to sleep in."

"You can sleep some other time. We are going to go to church today," she replied.

He bolted up in his bed and said, "Give me one good reason we need to go to church today."

"I'll give you *three* reasons," she replied. "First of all, it's good for you. Second, it's a habit in our family; we always go to church. And third, *you* are *the minister!*"

Now, that minister had lost something along the way. He forgot his commitment; he forgot the original challenge. That can so easily happen to us. We have not so much turned our backs on Christian commitment as we have forgotten it. We have not so much denied Christ as we have ignored him. We have not so much rejected Christianity as we have neglected it. Since we haven't been dramatically challenged, we have given our energies to other things. We all can sympathize, I am sure, with the woman who met a salesman at her door. He gave his pitch on the benefits of a new home freezer that he could provide, finally pointing out, "Ma'am, if you buy this freezer from me, you could save enough on food bills to pay for it." At this, the woman responded, "Mister, we are buying a car on the bus fare we save; we are paying for the washer on the laundry bills we save; and we are purchasing the house on the rent we save. To tell you the truth, we just can't afford to save any more right now."

Well, that's where most of us are in our faith pilgrimage. We know it's a good thing, but we are so strung out with so many other things that our energy is depleted. We have so many things to do and see about that we don't think we have any energy left or time left or creativity left for the single most important thing in our lives, namely, our relationship with God. Our faith has gotten crowded out in the ordinary times; our commitment has been elbowed into the background. We include the church in our lives when we can work it in, if it is convenient.

But the writer of Hebrews tells us to remember the earlier days. Remember what once challenged you; recall what once claimed your loyalty. Open the pages back to that chapter of your life that once captured your imagination and stirred your soul and energy for Christ. Recall the best that is in you. Look deeply for what has somehow gotten covered over and let it out to guide your life again.

That's the first thing the author of Hebrews says to us—remember the original challenge, and with God's help, keep it in your life daily.

Second, Remember the Ongoing Commitments of Discipleship

"Do not throw away your confidence," the writer says. Remember your commitment; stand for something lest you fall for everything. Once we have uncovered that which is vital to life, we have to work hard to hold on to it.

The great commitment is so much easier than the daily one. "Talking a good game" is not enough. We have to live it; we have to seize it; we have to celebrate it; we have to follow it. It is easier to make a commitment than it is to keep it; it is easier to plan a journey than it is to take it; it is easier to declare a loyalty than it is to practice it; it is easier to pay tribute to goodness than it is to pursue it.

Some years ago, I was asked to speak one Tuesday evening to an Alcoholics Anonymous group. Just before I was introduced, the chairman called on a man in the group to tell his story. The man, who was in his seventies, spoke powerfully about his life and the numerous tragedies caused by his drinking. Then he ended by speaking of his commitment to sobriety: "I've been sober now for fourteen years, and I'm committed to staying that way." He concluded with this interesting remark: "Getting sober is easy. I've done it hundreds and hundreds of times. It's *staying* sober that counts."

Precisely so. It's easy to make commitments. The hard thing is *keeping* them.

This brings me to the final suggestion.

Third, Remember the Ever-present Cost of Discipleship

Remember the ever-present cost of discipleship and remember to pay the price. Don't just flow with the stream. Don't just glide with the current. The writer of Hebrews says, "You have need of endurance, so that you may do the will of God" (10:36 RSV).

She was a delightful woman and very well advanced in years. She had purchased a small booklet the day before for twenty-five cents, and she liked it so much that she came back to buy another one for a friend of hers. As the clerk fixed her package, the woman noticed that the price of the booklet was now thirty-five cents. "But I only paid *a quarter* yesterday," she remarked.

"No, Ma'am," the clerk answered, "the price has been the same all week—thirty-five cents. I mark the books myself."

So the woman dug the rest of the cost from the bottom of her purse, saying, "Sorry I was such a bother," and she turned to leave.

The man behind her stepped up to the cash register, but then the woman turned back, stepped in front of him, and said, "I'm terribly sorry to interrupt, but there's one more thing I need to take care of with this young woman." The woman laid her handbag down on the counter and began to search it as best she could. "I hate to be such a bother but this is important," she said, as she smiled back at the growing line of people at the cash register.

The search continued but with no luck. Finally she put down her shawl and her packages and got both hands in her purse and searched and searched. Then, she found what she had been searching for, and out from the bottom of her handbag was lifted a single coin—a dime. Handing it to the clerk, she said, "This is for yesterday. I only paid you twenty-five cents for my booklet yesterday, so I owe you another dime."

"Oh, no, that's all right," the clerk said, trying to refuse the dime.

But the woman was insistent. "Oh, you must accept it. It's the only honest thing to do."

A big, gruff-looking man standing in line with a cigar in his mouth spoke up: "You're right, little lady. It always pays to be honest."

"Oh, no," the woman answered, stuffing the other items back into her purse. "No, it *costs* to be honest. It just cost me a dime; but Jesus is honest, and I try my best to be like him."

There was a glint from a tear in the eye of the clerk as she rang up the cash register.

Ten cents; one thin dime. Ten cents. Too many of us lose our standards or water down our commitments when life is just ordinary. Too many of us, too often, just drift in the stream. The writer of Hebrews tells us not to be like that. He tells us not to throw away what we know is right but rather to endure and do the will of God.

Honesty costs. Discipleship costs. Christianity costs in ordinary day-to-day living because it means what that woman knew. It means "being like Jesus," and trying to be like Jesus is what makes the most ordinary times extraordinary. So it is important—vitally important—to seize the day and live faithfully now.

CHAPTER THREE

You Can't Take It with You, So Live Peacefully Now

The Most Godlike Thing in the World

SCRIPTURE: MATTHEW 5:1-12

One of the things that fascinates me in baseball is how the coaches position their players on the field.

- When a power hitter comes up, they move them in the direction of his power.
- If a spray hitter comes to bat, they move the players in the other direction.
- And sometimes, they play them straight away.
- If the coaches expect the hitter to bunt, they pull the players up close.
- And they place them midway when they hope to turn a double play.
- In the later innings, the coaches move everybody way back to avoid an extra-base hit.

Coaches will tell you convincingly that close games are often won or lost just by the positioning of the players. A particular play can succeed or fail because of where the players are positioned. It's true in all sports. Positioning is all-important.

Positioning is tremendously important, also, in the game of life. And in the seventh beatitude (see Matthew 5:9) Jesus is saying to us: "Here's your position! Go into life as peacemakers! Let that be your stance! Let that be your attitude, your commitment! Take the position of peacemakers!"

Now, let me dissect this and bring it closer to home for us. Let me list some important qualities that I have found to be dramatically and radiantly present in the peacemakers I know.

First of All, I've Noticed That Peacemakers Are Patient People

When we study the Scriptures we realize pretty quickly that one of God's greatest qualities is God's patience. Over and over, time and again, God patiently forgives. God knows our weaknesses; God sees our sins; God is very much aware of our clay feet. And yet with amazing patience God keeps on forgiving us, loving us, and encouraging us.

The seventh beatitude challenges us to imitate God's patient ways. The late Ruth Graham was the wife of the well-known evangelist Billy Graham. Some years ago she decided what she wanted written on her tombstone when she died. It's not what you would expect at all—a most unusual statement indeed. She saw it one day on a road sign when she and her husband were driving on an interstate highway. They had driven through several miles of road construction. They had to slow down, often driving in single lanes of traffic and making short detours here and there.

Finally, they came to the end of the construction zone, and there Ruth Graham saw it—the sign that caught her attention. Pointing to the sign, she said to Dr. Graham, "Look! That's what I want on my tombstone!" At first, he didn't get it, but then it began to dawn on him and he smiled. The sign read: "End of Construction. Thank You for Your Patience."

Isn't that something? "End of Construction. Thank You for Your Patience." Those were the words Ruth Graham said she wanted on her tombstone!

Actually that would be a pretty accurate summary for all of our lives, wouldn't it?

We all have feet of clay.

We all have our shortcomings, our foibles, and our inadequacies.

We all mess up from time to time.

Every now and then, we all blow it.

We all stumble and fall.

We are all still under construction, and we all need God and people to be patient with us.

So why not just recognize that and turn that coin over and be patient with other people?

Why not take that stance?

Why not be a bridge builder?

Why not be an avid agent of reconciliation?

Why not imitate the gracious patience of God?

Why not be a patient peacemaker?

It's a Godlike thing to do.

Second, I've Noticed That Peacemakers Are Loving People

Have you heard about the young husband who complained to his new wife, "Why can't you make pie crust like my mother makes?" The wife answered, "Maybe I *could*, if you made 'dough' like my daddy makes!"

Whether it's a husband giving his wife a hard time, or a man pushing people out of the way so he can board an airplane first, or a child calling her mother an ugly name in a cafeteria line, or those insecure people who try to force their way and their ideas on everybody they meet, or a military tyrant aggressively and cruelly invading another country, disrespect for others is not a pretty picture! Hostility toward others is not a pretty picture. It is ungodly behavior, and peacemakers don't act that way!

Some years ago, one of our finest church members died. His name was George. Everybody loved George because he was a peacemaker. He had a big heart and a wonderful sense of humor. He used to say that he was so tenderhearted that he cried at supermarket openings! He worked at Methodist Hospital, and he was deeply loved both at church and at work because he was so kind and respectful toward every person he met.

A few days before George died, the president of Methodist Hospital stopped by George's hospital room to see him. They had a nice visit. As the hospital president left, one of the hospital janitors came in to see George. They too had a good visit. When the janitor left, one of George's children said to him, "Dad, did you realize that you treated the president of the hospital and the janitor just alike?" George smiled, and with a chuckle he said, "Let me ask you something. If the president left for two weeks and the janitor left for two weeks, which one would you miss the most?"

But then George said to his children, "Come over here and let me show you something that I carry in my pocket all the time. Even when I mow the lawn, I have these two things in my pocket." With that, he pulled out his pocket cross and his Golden Rule marble. He said, "On the cross are written these words: 'God loves you'; and on the marble are these words: 'Do unto others as you would have them do unto you.'" And then George said, "The cross reminds me of how deeply God loves me, and the marble reminds me of how deeply God wants me to love others."

What George was saying was this: "This is my position, my life stance, symbolized by a little silver cross and a red Golden Rule marble. I just want to let the love of God flow through me and out to others."

That's what it means to be a peacemaker, and that's what Saint Francis meant when he prayed, "Lord, make me an instrument of Thy peace; / where there is hatred, let me sow love; / where there is injury, pardon."

Over the years, scholars have come at the seventh beatitude, "Blessed are the peacemakers," from three different directions. Some have said it has to do with the Hebrew word *shalom*. *Shalom* means "wholeness, fullness, everything you need to make life good." So in that context, this beatitude could be paraphrased like this: "Blessed are those who work to improve the quality of life for everyone and who make this world a better place to live." This is what Abraham Lincoln meant when he said, "Die when I may, I would like it to be said of me that I always pulled up a weed and planted a flower where I thought a flower would grow."

Other scholars have suggested that the seventh beatitude has to do with inner peace, peace within, serenity in our hearts and souls.

Still other Bible scholars say this beatitude challenges us to work harder on our relationships with others. That's what it's all about, they say—being in right relationship with other people.

I'm sure it means some of all of these. I'm equally sure that the real peacemakers are people of patience and that they are people of love.

Finally and Most Important, Peacemakers Are Christlike People

But how do we find the spirit of Christ? How do we get what the Apostle Paul called "the mind of Christ"? Dr. Fred Craddock tells a beautiful story that helps us here.

Dr. Craddock was invited to the home of an older couple whose names were Nora and Frank. Dr. Craddock had preached in their church, and then Nora had brought him home for Sunday lunch. Her husband hadn't made it to church because he had shingles.

When they arrived, Frank was sitting in a rocking chair in front of the fireplace. He was in his eighties. Nora introduced Dr. Craddock to Frank, and then she went into the kitchen to prepare lunch. This conversation took place.

Dr. Craddock spoke first: "Well, Frank, how are you feeling?"

"Terrible."

"I understand you have shingles."

"Yep! Shingles. It's awful. Don't see how I can stand it much longer."

"You still have the pain?"

"Oh, yeah. It's constant pain."

"Well, how long have you had this, Frank?"

"Oh, I don't know. I've had it ever since last October or November. I don't remember which."

Then Frank shouted out, "Nora! Was it October or November?"

From the kitchen, Nora, without having heard any other portions of the conversation between Dr. Craddock and Frank, replied, "November."

Then Frank repeated to Dr. Craddock, "Since last November."

Later at the lunch table, Dr. Craddock asked, "Nora, how in the world did you know what he was talking about? When he yelled out October or November, how did you know what he meant?"

Nora just smiled and said, "Dr. Craddock, we've been married for fifty-three years!"

Wasn't that beautiful? She just knew, because she was "tuned in" to Frank.

If we live with somebody in a loving, trusting relationship over a period of time, we begin to think like that other person. It doesn't have to be fifty-three years, but if we spend enough quality time with Christ, we take on the mind of Christ. If we spend enough time with the Son of God, we become real children of God. If we spend enough time with the Prince of Peace, we will become peacemakers! And that's why it is so important to live peacefully now!

CHAPTER FOUR

You Can't Take It with You, So Live Victoriously Now

Beating Depression

SCRIPTURE: PSALM 42

At a church conference a few years ago, I walked into the bookstore one morning and found a minister friend of mine holding a book in his hand, looking at the title, and shaking his head sadly. The book was entitled something like *The Frustrating Problems and Intense Pressures Facing Today's Minister.* Looking up, he said to me, "Well, this is one book I don't need to read. I know about the problems and pressures of the ministry. I could write the book on those!"

In a way, that's the way we feel about depression. We all know what depression is. We could write the book on it. Sometimes we call it the blues or the blahs or feeling down and out; we all know the experience. Some call it "the slough of despond." Others call it "the dark night of the soul." The military call it "battle fatigue." The psychiatrist calls it "anxiety neurosis." The layman calls it "being down in the dumps" or "the pits."

But the psalmist, not knowing those names, simply said, "Out of the depths have I cried unto thee, O LORD" (Psalm 130:1 KJV); "Why art thou cast down, O my soul? And why art thou disquieted within me?" (Psalm 42:11 KJV). We have all known and felt the agony of feeling blue or blah or depressed. The question is, where does it come from? What causes it? And how do we deal with it creatively? How do we go about getting up and out of the depths of a depressed spirit?

Well, first let's focus on *the diagnosis*; let's diagnose the situation. Let's look together at some of the causes of depression and then we'll look at some of the Christian pointers toward a remedy or solution. What causes us to feel depressed? What drags us down to the point where we feel drained and defeated, tired and worn? Depression; how does it happen? Let me list several ideas, and I'm sure you will think of others.

First of All, Physical Problems Can Cause Depression

We are whole persons. God made us that way—body, mind, and spirit. Physical, mental, emotional, spiritual—they go together. We are all of one piece. What affects the one greatly influences the other. It is a fact that sometimes depression is caused by tiredness or lack of sleep, by an infection or a chemical deficiency, or by weight loss or a glandular imbalance. Physical problems like these can send us into an emotional tailspin that covers us over with a heavy blanket of depression.

Second, Depression Can Be Caused by Tension, the Tension of a Hectic World

In a real sense, you could say that our world's three major killers are not heart disease, cancer, and accidents, but rather calendars, telephones, and clocks—the tyranny of an accelerated life that we are all caught up in these days.

Some years ago, Dr. J. Wallace Hamilton wrote a sermon that he called "A Quiet Heart." At the beginning of that sermon, he told of a time in Chicago when the Heart Association did a fascinating thing. They asked a group of doctors to do a program for the leading businesspeople of Chicago, the "movers and shakers" of that busy city. The doctors, in presenting their program, used a graphic display. They placed before these wheeler-dealer executives of Chicago four large glass containers. Strangely, in each of the jars was a human heart, preserved in whatever doctors use to preserve such things.

The first heart was that of a man who had died in an accident, and it was exactly as a heart should appear in a man of middle years.

The second heart was swollen, enlarged to almost twice its normal size. It was the heart of a hot-tempered, hard-driving businessman who was very arrogant and very aggressive and who had died in a fit of temper while arguing with a client.

The third heart had belonged to a man who had lived under continual tension, refusing to relax or delegate responsibility. He had died from a coronary thrombosis.

The fourth heart displayed had belonged to a man who, along in middle life, under the strain of domestic trouble, had suffered a heart attack; but he had recovered and had come back to enjoy many more years of normal living.

Now, this graphic object lesson of four hearts was so traumatic to those business leaders in the audience that it slowed down business for a whole week in the city of Chicago (J. Wallace Hamilton, *What about Tomorrow?* [Old Tappan, NJ: Revell, 1972], 101-2).

The tensions of our pressure-packed and hectic way of life can affect our hearts physically, but they also can affect our hearts emotionally; and they can drag us down into the depths of depression.

Third, Depression Can Come from Feeling Rejected

The feeling of rejection, whether it's real or imagined, is one of the most devastating blows to human personality. We see it illustrated in the parable of the prodigal son. We see there a depressed elder brother.

Remember the story about the Sunday-school teacher who asked her fifth-grade class, "Who was sad and depressed when the prodigal son returned home?" A little boy in the back of the room answered, "The fatted calf?"

Maybe so, but the answer she was looking for was the elder brother. He was so depressed because he felt profoundly rejected. In fact, I would venture to guess that the prodigal son's return would not have upset the elder brother so much if it had been different. If the prodigal son had come slinking back into the household as a sorry, desperate, apologetic young man, placed on probation for a while to be sure he had learned his lesson, that would have been one thing. But the elder brother came unglued when he found the younger brother being received like a celebrity: he was given a new suit, new shoes, the family ring, a beef barbecue, live music—and the whole town was invited.

This was too much to stomach! The elder brother felt jealous. He felt sorry for himself. But even worse, he felt that their father had rejected him. Of course, the father *hadn't* rejected him, but the elder brother *felt* rejected, and it absolutely deflated him.

The feeling of rejection can pull the rug out from under the strongest of us. It's undoubtedly sometimes the reason a marriage ends in divorce, and divorce is for some people more traumatic than losing someone to death. If your mate dies you feel the hurt and loneliness, but the trauma of divorce carries with it also the feeling of rejection, the feeling of being unwanted, discarded, not needed.

That same kind of trauma is part of what happens to a prisoner. The prisoner feels caged; set apart; walled out and rejected by society. Sometimes older folk are made to feel that way in our youth-oriented culture, and that sense of rejection can produce heavy depression. Then too, when tragedy strikes, some people don't understand and they feel as if God has rejected them. Of course, God hasn't rejected them, but they *feel* that way, and that can be very depressing.

Now, there are many other causes of depression, such as ethical conflict, hereditary influences and other medical conditions, shock, grief, disillusionment, prolonged illness, disappointments, significant life changes, or some sort of identity crisis. Some psychiatrists have defined depression as "frozen rage," suggesting that it comes from unresolved, unexpressed, or undealt with anger.

All of these are significant, but let me mention one other cause of depression that I think is more dramatic than we may realize.

It's What I Call (for Want of a Better Term) the Depression That Comes from Being Spiritually Hungry

I have to confess to you that personally I am more prone to the blahs when I have drifted away from God. Depression is a signal for me that I am hungry for God.

Some weeks ago, I was driving home late one evening after an unusually hectic and draining day. All of a sudden, it hit me. I felt so blue, so sad, so depleted, so depressed. I realized that I was feeling sorry for myself. My mind darted back to a panel discussion I had participated in a few days before. I was on the panel with a medical doctor, a teacher, a lawyer, and a psychiatrist. Someone asked this brilliant psychiatrist what he does when he feels depressed. He smiled and said, "I talk to myself. I try to analyze my situation objectively by asking myself just why I am depressed. If we can get in touch with what is causing the depression, then we can deal with it creatively and productively."

I decided to try it. I asked myself, "Well, Jim, what is it that is making you feel so bad?" As I looked back over the day, I remembered that I felt fine that morning. I couldn't recall being rejected or hurt in any way during the day. Then, it hit me. I realized that I had been so busy that I had neglected to eat breakfast, lunch, and dinner. My problem was that I was hungry, and my body was sending me a signal. Later, when I got home and had a good meal, I felt just fine! It struck me that evening as I thought back over it, that this was a parable for our spiritual lives. If missing a meal physically can depress us, just think what it must do to us when we get *spiritually* hungry. I am amazed at how people make it without the church, because I need the church so very much that I get spiritually hungry. And when I drift away from God, when I neglect my prayer life, when I slip away from my study of the Scriptures, when I miss out on Sunday school, when I get away from the Christian community, I find myself so much more susceptible to self-pity and depression.

It's interesting to note that many great people in church history went through periods of deep depression just before they made significant breakthroughs that brought them closer to God and changed the history of the world.

Think about it. Martin Luther was depressed for years because he was "scared to death" of God. But then, as he studied the Apostle Paul's words in Romans about "justification by faith," he "broke through" and realized that God loved him already, that he didn't have to win God's love. Luther basked in the glow of that discovery. He was so hungry for God's love, and his discovery of it started the Protestant Reformation.

John Wesley was so hungry for God that he was greatly depressed. He couldn't seem to get close to God, but then came the "warming of his heart" at Aldersgate, and the Methodist movement was on its way. And I can imagine Moses brooding out on the hillside just moments before he experienced God in the burning bush and was sent to bring the people called Israel out of bondage.

I can see Paul trudging somberly down the Damascus Road, troubled, burdened, thinking deep thoughts, when God exploded into his life so powerfully that Paul and the whole world would never ever be the same again. Isaiah, Jeremiah, and Hosea—all were depressed because they were spiritually hungry. They were hungry for God, and when they found God, God made them prophets.

All throughout history we see it—people hungry for God. Remember how Augustine put it: "Our hearts are restless till they find rest in Thee." I am convinced that one of the first questions we need to ask when we feel depressed is this one: Have I drifted away from God? And is this depression a signal for me that I am thirsting for God like that thirsty hart in the Psalm 42? Am I hungry for God like Luther, Wesley, Moses, Paul, and Isaiah were?

As we have seen, all kinds of things can cause depression. But what is the remedy? What is the solution? Let me pause here for a moment to say that if you are suffering from severe depression or believe that you may be, please consult your doctor. The following guidelines are not intended as a substitute for medical care, but rather they are simple, helpful suggestions for handling the everyday blues and blahs when they come.

First, Remember That It Is Temporary

Don't accept the mood of depression as permanent. Remember that this too will pass. Right now, you may be under a cloud; but let me tell you the sun is still shining. It's just that the cloud is in the way at the moment blocking the sunshine. Before long the cloud will pass on and you'll be out in the sunlight again. So the first thing to remember is that the mood of depression is not permanent. It is temporary, and it will pass.

Second, Talk It Out with Somebody

There is an interesting old saying that makes a good point. It goes like this: "What the average patient wants is not a doctor, but an audience." All of us, from time to time, need to talk out our problems, and one of the most therapeutic things we can do is sit down with a trusted friend and verbalize what's bothering us. So when you feel blue, talk it out with somebody, and talk it out with God.

Third, Learn to Laugh; Cultivate a Sense of Humor

Don't take yourself so seriously. To be able to laugh at yourself is one of the greatest marks of emotional and spiritual maturity, and how desperately we need it.

A minister friend of mine loves to tell about the time he was stopped by a policeman in Houston. He said to the officer, "Please don't give me a ticket. I'm just a poor preacher."

"I know, I know," said the policeman, "I heard you preach last Sunday!"

My friend tells that story with obvious delight!

Some years ago on Memorial Day I was asked to speak at a special citywide memorial service. The man coordinating the event said to me, "Jim, you speak first, and then the firing squad will come after you"!

The single quality we need perhaps more than any

other is the ability to laugh at ourselves. A. Powell Davies said it powerfully:

> When we see our grotesqueries, how quaint we are, how droll our ambitions are, how comical we are in almost all respects, we automatically become more sane, less self-centered, more humble, more wholesome. To laugh at ourselves, we have to stand outside ourselves—and that is an immense benefit. Our puffed-up pride and touchy self-importance vanish; a clean and sweet humility begins to take possession of us. We are on the way to growing a soul. (Arthur Powell Davies, *The Mind and Faith of A. Powell Davies*, ed. William Orville Douglas [Garden City, NY: Doubleday, 1959], 209.)

Oh how we need to learn to laugh! And oh how we need to learn to laugh at ourselves!

Fourth, Forget Yourself into Usefulness

Isn't that a great thought? Forget yourself into usefulness. It's the title of a chapter in Dr. Frank Caprio's classic book *Living in Balance*. Dr. Caprio dedicated the book to his mother who he said taught him how to live in balance with an ancient Latin proverb: *Labor et amour omnia vincit*, which means, "Work and love conquer everything."

How true it is. When you feel blue, reach out and touch someone else with love. When you feel down, the quickest way to get up is to go help someone else, to get outside yourself, to forget yourself into usefulness. It's the best therapy in the world for getting over depression.

Fifth and Finally, Lean on God

Remember how the psalmist said it: "Why are you cast down, O my soul? and why are you disquieted within me?" (Psalm 42:11). But notice that he doesn't stop there. No, he says, "Hope in God; for I shall again praise [God], my help and my God."

That's the answer, isn't it? For us to recognize that God is not some computer, off somewhere in the foggy distance. God is with us here. God is beside us now. God is within us. God is for us. God is our loving Parent, and nothing can separate us from God and God's love.

Read the Bible closely and you will discover that the thread that holds it all together is the love of God. God loves us. God is with us. God will not desert us. God will save us and heal us.

I have a friend whose Bible is filled with notes in the margins. By some verses she has written, simply, "T. P." When asked what T. P. means, she says, "tried and proved."

When you feel depressed, nothing helps more than remembering that you can lean on God and God's love and strength. You see, it's "T. P." It's tried and proved!

CHAPTER FIVE

You Can't Take It with You, So Live Boldly Now

Use It or Lose It

SCRIPTURE: MATTHEW 25:14-29

I am a collector of lists. One of my all-time favorites is a list of answers given by English schoolchildren on their religion exam. One student wrote, "Noah's wife was called Joan of the ark." Another said, "A *myth* is a female moth." Still another said, "The fifth commandment is 'Humor your father and mother.'" And one student wrote, "Sometimes you can't hear in church because the *agnostics* are so terrible." (There's a sermon there somewhere!) But my favorite one of all is this last one. One student wrote these words, and let me quote them precisely: "Lot's wife was a pillar of salt by day, and a ball of fire by night!"

Now, give those children an E for effort. They are trying to get at the truth.

I want to try to get at the truth of one of the strangest verses in the entire Bible. The scripture from Matthew

25:29 at first glance may be confusing. Some people would list this as one of the most perplexing verses in the Bible: "For to all those who have, more will be given, and they will have an abundance; but from those who have nothing, even what they have will be taken away." What does this mean? Why give more to the one who has plenty and take away from the one who has so little? It sounds so unfair, and for that reason the verse is a frustrating mystery to many people.

To unravel the mystery, it helps to see the verse in context. It comes at the end of Jesus' parable of the talents. Jesus told the story of how a man was going on a journey. Before leaving, the man called in three of his servants. He left five talents (units of money) with one servant. He left two talents with another servant, and he entrusted one talent to still another servant, and then he went away.

During the man's absence the servant with five talents traded with his and made five more; and the servant with two talents used his to earn two more; but the servant with one talent buried his talent in the ground for safekeeping because he was afraid. He was afraid of his master, afraid of failure, afraid to take a risk, afraid to try; and so, paralyzed by his fear, he did nothing. He buried his talent in the ground.

When the master returned, he commended the two servants who had used their gifts and increased them. But when the one-talent servant came in for the accounting, the master became quite upset with him because he had done nothing. The master rebuked him, calling him "wicked" and "slothful." But more than that, he took away this servant's one talent and gave it to the servant who now had ten talents. Then comes that haunting verse: "For to all those who have, more will be given, and they will have an abundance; but from those who have nothing, even what they have will be taken away."

What is this all about? The key that unlocks this is to understand that the true meaning stands out when we see that Jesus is not talking about money. He is not talking about bank stocks or real estate. Rather, he is talking about our abilities, our talents, our capabilities, our gifts, and our inner determination to use what we have! Jesus is underscoring a fascinating and dependable principle of life, namely, that if we don't use our gifts and talents, we lose them. If we don't use our abilities, they shrivel and die. The truth of that principle is as wide as life itself. Ask any athlete or musician; any artist or scholar; any salesperson or surgeon; any writer or preacher.

Each in his or her own way will tell you that he or she has learned from his or her own experience that it is true: we either use our talents or we lose them! This principle literally pervades every area of life.

The Physical Level

We all know it is true on the physical level that our talents, capabilities, and gifts are enhanced, improved, and increased by use, exercise, and practice. This is what gives the sailor his keen eye, the pianist her nimble wrist, the surgeon his deft hand, and the runner her grace and endurance. Jesus is so right—the one who has the will and determination to exercise and use his or her talents physically, increases them.

We can also see in the physical world the other side

of the coin: if we *don't* use our abilities, we lose them. For example, some species of moles that live underground have eyes, but cannot see; and the fish that swim in Echo River in Mammoth Cave have become, over many generations, eyeless. They neglected to use what they had, and nature took its natural revenge. The underground moles and the Mammoth Cave fish once had eyes that appeared outwardly perfect, but over time they lost the ability to see because of lack of use! Whether you are dealing with fish or moles or people, the principle holds true: either use it or you lose it.

Some years ago, professional golfer Byron Nelson was winning all the major golf tournaments. He played with such perfect precision that he was called the "mechanical man" of the fairways. But then he retired from the pro tour and came to live on his ranch in Texas. The few times when he emerged from his retirement to play again, he simply was no match for the leaders. He had proved long ago and many times over that he had the talent, by winning so regularly on the tour; but when he stopped, he lost the competitive edge, and he lost the power to win.

This principle is dramatically true on the physical level. If we use our talents, we enhance them.

Happy Chandler was the governor of Kentucky for many years. He was asked late in his life what was the key to his long life and good health. He gave an interesting answer. He said that early on in his marriage, his wife and he made an agreement. They decided that every time he got upset with her, rather than argue, he would walk around the backyard in the open air until he calmed down. A questioner asked, "How did that help?" Happy Chandler, with a twinkle in his eye, responded that forty-five years of exercise in the open air could make a person really healthy! Some years ago, I was a pretty good athlete. I made All-Memphis twice in basketball. I made the all-district and all-regional teams in Tennessee, and I received honorable mention on some of the all-state teams in Tennessee. I averaged twenty-two points per game my senior year in high school and went to college on an athletic work scholarship. But a few years ago I embarrassed myself silly in a basketball game. It was United Methodist Day on the Centenary College campus. Children's choirs sang, the bishop was presented with a special gift from the college, and a group of ministers was asked to play a fifteen-minute basketball game during halftime of the Centenary-Southern Methodist University game. I played, and this is what happened: my mind said, *Intercept that pass, dribble full speed down the court, fake out the defender, dribble behind your back, and soar high for a crowd-pleasing, double-pump, swooping reverse, left-hand layup.* That's what my mind said to my body. My body answered back, *Who? Me?* My mind said, *Yes, you. You can do it. You've done it before, and you can do it now. Go to it.* That's what my mind said to my body. My body answered back, *You gotta be kiddin'!*

My body refused to respond because it hadn't been used that way in so long. I hadn't exercised; I hadn't practiced; I hadn't played; and it was awful. I did pretty well for about thirty seconds, and after that it was terrible! I was the third most embarrassed person in that arena; the two most embarrassed were our children, who kept saying repeatedly to their mother, "Just think, after this is over, he's actually going to come over here and sit down beside us."

I learned the hard way that Saturday afternoon the agonizing truth of this principle: if you don't use it, you lose it.

The Intellectual Level

It's also true on the intellectual level. If we work at it, if we stretch our minds, they grow. But if we put our minds into neutral and stop learning, our minds shrivel up on us.

We tend to think that some people are smart and others are not. The truth is that the difference is not so much in wisdom or brain capacity as it is in hard work. The good students are not just those who are smart. They are the ones who work at it, the ones willing to pay the price.

Henry Wadsworth Longfellow expressed it well in his poem "The Ladder of St. Augustine":

The heights by great men reached and kept,
Were not attained by sudden flight,
But they, while their companions slept,
Were toiling upward in the night.

Hard work does it.

In the British Museum in London, the original pages used by Thomas Gray in writing his now-famous poem "Elegy Written in a Country Churchyard" are on display. There are seventy-five drafts of that one poem. Gray wrote it, but didn't quite like it. He wrote it a second time and it was still not quite right, so he rewrote it. He rewrote it seventy-five times before he got it into the form we now read.

Some years ago, a young boy came from a poor farm

in Canada to America to become a minister. He never went to seminary; he couldn't afford it. He took a church in Baileyton, Tennessee. After a short time there, he went to pastor a church in Saint Petersburg, Florida. The day he arrived, the church had forty-six members and an average attendance of thirty-four. The first Sunday's offering was $5.76. When he died forty years later, he was still serving the same church, but the membership was close to four thousand and the average congregation each Sunday was more than twenty-five hundred. He was known and respected as one of the finest preaching voices of our time and the author of several top-selling books. How could this be? How did J. Wallace Hamilton do it?

The answer, of course, is work—hard work. J. Wallace Hamilton kept studying, stretching his mind, and trying to improve. First of all, and beyond everything else, hard work did it for him.

Physically it is true and intellectually it is true: either we use it or we lose it.

The Social Level

It's also true on the social level. If we learn how to interact with people, we can do pretty well. But if we go into seclusion and shut people out of our lives, we can get into trouble.

Sandra is a friend of mine. She was in high school, a member of our church, and an active leader in our youth group. She was bright, outgoing, attractive, popular, and she loved people. When Sandra finished college, she began to struggle with the call to the ministry. She thought God might be calling her into the ministry but she wasn't sure. Since she had saved quite a bit of money and didn't have to work, she decided to go into seclusion for one year to study, pray, meditate, and listen for God's call. She wanted to separate herself from any outside distractions, so she refused to use the telephone; she would not answer the door; she didn't go outside of her house; she would not see anybody. All she did was study. She had no television, no radio, no newspapers—no contact with the outside world.

Several months into the experiment her mother called and asked me to go with her to Sandra's home. She said, "Something has happened to Sandra. This secluded lifestyle has changed her. She needs help. You'll have to see it to believe it." We went together to Sandra's home. I couldn't believe my eyes. When Sandra heard us coming, she was terrified. She ran to the back of the house to hide from us. She was hiding behind the drapes, peeping out fearfully with a panicked look on her face, scared to death to face another human being.

It was obvious what she needed. She needed to get back into the world, back into society, and I'm happy to report she is now doing well. But the point is clear: it's true socially as well as physically and intellectually—we use it or we lose it.

The Spiritual Level

If it's true that practice makes perfect in music, golf, art, poetry, speaking, writing, and even relating to others, it must be true that practice enhances the spiritual graces. If you want to have a good prayer life, there is only one way to do it—you just pray, pray, and pray some more. You have to work at it.

If you want to have a good grasp of the Bible, there is only one way. You study the Scriptures. Study, study, and study some more. Then read the dictionaries and commentaries, and everything you can get your hands on about the Bible. That is the only way to do it.

If you want to be a good churchperson, how do you do it? You get in the stream of the church and you go every time the doors of the church open. You get involved and you participate; you go expectant, hoping, learning it, and living it.

How do you become a good Christian? You live it, every day. You practice living the Christian life until you get it right. We either live the faith or we lose it. Every time we say no to God, the longer we put God off, the more difficult it becomes to say yes to God. And the more we say yes to God, the easier it becomes to say yes to God and to life.

That's the choice that is open to us, spiritually, in our faith experience. We use it or we lose it. So, the point is clear and obvious: live boldly now.

CHAPTER SIX

You Can't Take It with You, So Live Courageously Now

Rising above Disillusionment and Disappointment

SCRIPTURE: HEBREWS 10:23-25

The middle-aged woman sitting across from me was crestfallen. She was burdened, confused, heartbroken, and scared. Her husband of more than twenty years had suddenly died three months before. Now, she had come to the church because the grief pains of that loss were eating her up, gnawing away at her incessantly. "I still cry a lot," she said to me, "especially late at night. I feel so alone, so afraid, so unable to cope, and so disillusioned. When he died, it seemed like a big part of me died with him. My whole world was wrapped up in him, and now he is gone." She looked at the floor for a moment and then said, "What in the world am I going to do? I have faith. I love God and I trust God, but where is God now when I need God so desperately? I know God is out there somewhere, but somehow I feel like I have been jolted out of contact with the Lord."

I guess all of us can identify with that woman and the agonizing despair reflected in her words as she cried out for God. We have all known painful moments like that. This is the way it feels sometimes. We have faith. We believe. We try to live our faith daily. We trust God. But in spite of that, there are moments in our lives when we seem to lose our grip on life, when faith is hard to hold on to, when God seems far away.

Those difficult moments come for all of us when we feel disillusioned, disappointed, and downhearted. The problem of disillusionment is what I want us to focus on in this chapter.

There's a dramatic picture of it in the Gospel of Luke, in the Emmaus road story (see Luke 24:13-35). Remember Cleopas and Simon on the Emmaus road. It is Easter afternoon. They know about the Crucifixion having taken place, but they have not yet encountered the Resurrection. Disappointed, disillusioned, heartbroken, and downcast, they trudge down the Emmaus road toward home. Their hopes for the future dashed, they turn back toward the old life.

Picture them in your mind. Their shoulders are slumped. Their heads are bowed as though they carry on their backs a crushing burden of defeat and dejection. They trudge with weary steps as if their shoes are weighted with lead. Their eyes are misted over with the tears of disillusionment. They walk along in silence. They dare not speak for fear they will break into uncontrollable sobbing. At last, with a sigh filled with despair, the younger man speaks: "He's dead; he's gone; it's all over. They have killed him, and without him we are nothing. We should have known this wouldn't work. It was too good to be true, too idealistic for this cruel world. How could we have been such fools? We followed him. We trusted. We thought he was the one to save us."

That is the portrait of disillusionment. But we know the rest of the story: how the resurrected Lord comes and walks with them, how they return to Jerusalem to share the good news, and how in the process they too get resurrected. Before that encounter, however, they are a graphic sketch of disillusioned men.

Now the question is, how do we deal with disillusionment in a productive way? How do we handle disappointments creatively? How do we get "up" when we feel so downcast? How does a broken heart get mended? How do we keep the faith when it is difficult?

Let me tell you about Maida Mickle. She was one of my favorite people in the entire world. The first twenty years of her life she studied and prepared to serve God. The second twenty years of her life she spent as a missionary in China and Japan. The third twenty years of her life she gave herself in a signal way to one of our Methodist schools as the first lady of Centenary College. The next twenty years of her life she dedicated to a couples' Sunday-school class, and through her dedication and hard work quite simply made it one of the greatest Sunday-school classes in America.

She was a saint in the church—not a pious, puritanical saint, but a "salty saint," full of life, vigor, wit, and vibrancy. She had two favorite sayings, which help us find an answer to the problem of disillusionment. First, she said, "I would rather wear out than rust out!" And second, she said, "We have to keep on keeping on."

In essence, this was the answer those two disciples found on the Emmaus road: "We can't quit! We can't throw in the towel! We have to keep on keeping on!" Also, this is the way the writer of the book of Hebrews said it. He was writing to a people under heavy persecution. These people were tired and disillusioned. They were scared and confused. They were downcast and heartbroken. The writer knew it, and he wrote these words: "Let us hold fast the confession of our hope without wavering, for he who promised is faithful; and let us consider how to stir up one another to love and good works, not neglecting to meet together... but encouraging one another" (Hebrews 10:23-25 RSV).

In other words, the writer was saying, "Don't quit! Don't give up! Don't lose heart! Keep on keeping on!" When you feel disillusioned, disappointed, and downhearted, it helps to remember these words from the writer of Hebrews to the early church. They can help put the stars back in the sky for you.

Let's look at this more closely by breaking it down a bit. Here are three thoughts.

When You Feel Disillusioned, Disappointed, and Downhearted, Remember, First of All, to Keep on Loving Others

Recall how the writer put it. He said, "Let us... stir up one another to love and good works." He is so right. The best antidote for the poison of despair is to reach out and touch someone else with love. The best way to get over your problem is to get outside yourself, to forget yourself into usefulness. When people come to the church and say their faith is dwindling, the question I always want to ask is, Are you still serving God? It's hard to lose God when you are serving.

A woman came to see her minister one day. She was despondent. She was quite wealthy, but her money had not brought her happiness. She had found no meaning or purpose in life. She felt empty inside. Life had turned sour for her. She had come to the church now, seeking help. Her minister asked her, "Will you do whatever I ask you?"

"Yes," she answered.

The pastor said, "You are not going to want to do this, but if you will do it, it will change your life. Go and buy some flowers tomorrow morning. Then go down to the hospital for the poor. Go onto one of the wards and give the flowers to the patients there."

The woman didn't want to do that. She had never even been inside that hospital; it seemed beneath her. But because she had promised the minister, she went. She bought the flowers, went down to the hospital, climbed the stairs to the second ward, and began to hand out the flowers to those in the midst of pain and suffering and loneliness. It was embarrassing at first, but she found herself amazed at the way the patients' faces lit up as she handed them the flowers. She was touched by the gratitude that showed in their eyes and the willingness of many to talk to her because she was willing to listen.

The next week she went back again, and again the week after that. Soon she began going twice a week, and on and on it went for several years. She became known as "the flower lady" at that particular hospital, and she was able to bring into the lives of many people a little bit of beauty, joy, and love. But at the same time, *she* got well! She discovered for herself a new meaning, purpose, and joy in life. Her minister had been right. As she reached out to others with love, her disillusionment faded, and it was replaced by happiness and fulfillment. That's the way it is. Remember how Jesus said it: "When we lose ourselves for others, we find ourselves!" If we feel we have lost God, the way to find him again is to discover him by loving his children. So when we feel downcast, or if we feel our faith is slipping, the thing to do is to "keep on keeping on." The thing to do is to keep on loving others.

Second, When You Feel Disillusioned, Disappointed, and Downhearted, Remember to Keep on Encouraging Others

The writer of Hebrews reminds us that we are a family, a community of faith sharing the joys and sorrows of life together from the cradle to the grave. "Encourage one another," he says to us. We were never meant to bear our burdens by ourselves. It is the genius of the Christian faith that it recognizes this truth. You see, we solve our problems better in community than in isolation. We all need a support community—a support system to affirm us, to uphold us, to encourage us—and that is a significant part of the task of the church.

The Scriptures put it like this: "Bear ye one another's burdens" (Gal. 6:2). Tragically, many people make a bad mistake at this point. For example, remember the woman I mentioned earlier whose husband had died. Part of her problem was that she had stayed away from church. "The church was so special to us," she said, "I couldn't bear to come back without him." But, you see, that's a mistake. The church should be a part of the healing process. It's our support system; and when heartache comes, we need to get back to the church as quickly as we can.

Let me illustrate this personally. On December 17, 1979, my mother died instantly in an automobile accident in Winston-Salem, North Carolina. The funeral was held in Memphis on December 20. We had to stay over a few days longer to handle some family and business matters. We flew back into Shreveport, where we were living at the time, on Christmas Eve, still very much in shock and grieving deeply.

Our plane landed at 3:30 that Christmas Eve afternoon. We drove to our home, put our luggage inside the house, looked quickly at the mail, and then headed for the church for the Christmas Eve Communion service. This was a very emotional moment for me—our first time back in our church since Mother's funeral. I will never forget what happened that night as long as I live. It was one of the most moving spiritual experiences of my life.

As I moved up and down the altar rail, serving the bread tray, people reached out and touched my hands. They didn't say anything—they just touched my hands. Even now, my eyes water as I think of it. I had never had that happen before or since—hundreds of people just touching my hands, saying nothing verbally, but saying oh so much with the gentle touch of encouragement! It was a powerful moment for me. I had never felt more loved or more encouraged. Now, that is what the church is all about.

Whatever happens, we must keep on loving and keep on encouraging.

Third, When You Feel Disillusioned, Disappointed, and Downhearted, Remember, We Must Keep on Worshiping with Others

Remember the writer of Hebrews said not to neglect meeting together. Worship was what he was talking about, and he was right. When we get discouraged or feel defeated we need to get into the presence of God. Worship is our great reminder that God is with us, and nothing, not even death, can separate us from the Lord.

Isaiah went to the Temple one day crestfallen and downhearted. King Uzziah had died, and the people didn't know what would become of their nation. It was in danger of falling. There were all kinds of problems, and Isaiah was confused and scared and discouraged. So he went to the Temple and worshiped, and there he saw the Lord "high and lifted up" (Isaiah 6:1 RSV). He needed that. It reminded Isaiah that King Uzziah had died but that the King of Kings had not. The King of Kings was very much alive. God was still in control of things, and he could be trusted. That's what worship does for us.

Some time back, I ran across a true story that underscores the point. A chaplain in World War II told of a Sunday morning on one of the islands south of Japan. It was time for worship and it was raining badly, so hard that one could hardly see through it. Despite the rainstorms, about one hundred men gathered in the mud and the mire. This chaplain shouted over the noise of the rain and wind, "Do you want to have worship service today?" To the man, they all said yes. So they hummed some familiar hymns because they didn't have hymnbooks. They recited the familiar words of the twenty-third Psalm because they had no Bible. The chaplain said, "The rain was beating down on my steel helmet and the water was coming off, and I could hardly see them. I asked them, 'Do you want me to preach?'" Standing in the rain, ankle-deep in mud, the men answered back, "Yes, preach." So for twenty minutes, the chaplain preached to those men and they listened intently.

The chaplain later said that he came back to the civilian pulpit where people sit in cushioned pews and air-conditioned comfort, where there are those who feel that to come two blocks to church is a very painful thing to do. Why is it that a worship service over there in the mud and mire means more than worship in a beautiful church sanctuary sometimes? The answer is simple: those men on that rain-soaked island knew that they were facing the possibility of death at any moment, and they needed to be reminded that the God they put their faith in and trusted their lives with was bigger than the world, bigger than the war, bigger even than death, and as long as they put their trust in God, all was well.

We need to remember that week by week. So when times are hard, keep on keeping on; keep on loving, encouraging, trusting God; and keep on worshiping together.

CHAPTER SEVEN

You Can't Take It with You, So Live Triumphantly Now

You Can Cope

SCRIPTURE: LUKE 9:10-17

I have a friend who once told of a strange idea he had as a boy: he thought that he could outrun germs! Once, as a little boy, he came down with a terrible cold, and somehow he got the idea that if he could run fast from one room to another, he could run away from those germs the way he could run away from his puppy.

His mother found him dashing from room to room, all out of breath, and when she discovered what he was attempting to do, she gently but wisely called him back to reality. She explained that he couldn't outrun the germs; no matter where he ran or how fast he went the germs would go with him. "The sooner you quit trying to run away from your cold," she said, "and start doing what the doctor prescribed, the quicker you will get well."

There is a great truth here, not only for treating

colds, but also for dealing with all of life's problems; and yet we are so slow to learn that! We can't outrun our problems. The sooner we accept this fact and decide to face our problems, the better; and yet we are so slow to understand that. This incessant search for a way to escape the inescapable and the chronic resentment of the problems are an incredible waste of energy. And yet, if we are honest, we must confess that we have squandered a large portion of our lives running, hiding, fleeing, and escaping.

Some scholars have referred to our time as "the Age of Escapism." The reference may be indeed appropriate. Look at what is happening. For example, we've seen an increase in drug abuse. Now, let me ask you something. Why do people take drugs? Why do people use and abuse drugs?

Some people use drugs to "get high"—in other words, to get above and beyond their problems; but they ultimately crash, with more trouble than they started with in the first place. Some people take drugs so they can sleep, because if they can sleep then they can avoid their problems at least for a little while; but when they wake up, the problems are still there. Some people take drugs so they can relax, in the hope that somehow the tension might be released or eased; but still again, the tension returns, the uptightness comes back, the nerves stretch tighter—and sometimes they snap. Some people take drugs so they can get drunk. (Don't forget that alcohol is a drug.) They drink and drink and get drunk so they can forget their problems; but when they sober up, the troubles are still there, along with a terrific hangover. Some people take drugs so they can cope with life's problems. They say, "This pill will make me brave"; "This pill will calm me down"; "This pill will give me strength"; "This pill will settle my nerves." And it's all so ridiculous. It's all so absurd. All of these abuses and misuses of drugs are simply our childish attempts to outrun the germs, our infantile ways of trying to run away from or hide from our problems. But when will we ever learn that there is no escape from the problems of this world? Problems are here to stay. There are no problem-free jobs. There are no problem-free marriages. There are no problem-free homes. There are no problem-free communities. There are no problem-free churches. There are no problem-free worlds.

So, we really can't run away. We really can't escape. We have to face the problems; handle the difficulties; deal with the troubles. There is no hiding place. There is no place to run!

So we need to learn how to cope with our hardships creatively, productively, and meaningfully. Once again, our great teacher is Jesus. We see in him the model and the pattern for dealing with problems productively. In him, we see how to cope with difficulties in creative ways.

For example, look with me at one of the most famous events in Jesus' life, the time when he fed five thousand people in the wilderness. This episode must have made a deep impression on the disciples because it is the only miracle (not counting the Resurrection) in the whole ministry of Jesus that is recorded in all four Gospels.

The story was familiar to me when I looked at it again recently, but I was amazed to discover just how relevant it is to this particular issue of coping with life's difficulties. This story depicts Jesus up against a real down-to-earth problem, and the way he responded is fascinating and enlightening.

Jesus and his disciples were trying to get away by

themselves so they could reflect on the mission the Twelve had just completed. They were "getting away," not "running away"—and there's a big difference. Galilee was a crowded, densely populated region, so they had crossed the Sea of Galilee to the more private eastern shore. But the people, the crowds, had followed them.

One of the great things about Jesus was that he never looked upon needy human beings as a nuisance. Instead, out of his deep compassion, Jesus rearranged his plans and worked with these interruptions constantly and meaningfully.

Now, his *disciples* were more like *us*. They weren't so patient or understanding. They weren't so compassionate, gracious, generous, or creative. They were worn out. They were tired of the crowd, and they wanted to be rid of them. They also realized that the people were hungry and tired, and that crowds in this condition could get hostile and out of hand.

So, the disciples began to strategize. They pulled Jesus aside and pointed out the difficulty, suggesting that he disperse the people quickly before things went from bad to worse. It was a perfectly natural suggestion in the face of what Jesus and the disciples were facing— a problem situation, full of stress and potential danger.

But look closely at how Jesus proceeded to cope with the problem. And notice that his response is a beautiful model for us for coping with problems creatively. It can be outlined in three stages. Let's look at these more closely.

First, Jesus Chose to Cope Rather than Run

Jesus chose to face the situation rather than flee. He refused to follow the disciples' suggestion that they employ the strategy of escapism. He decided instead to face the situation squarely, openly, and confidently, trusting God to help bring him through it. Instead of saying, "Trouble is coming; let's go our way and let them go theirs," he said, "We are involved in this event together. We cannot pass the buck. Let's face it and deal with it." Then, with the help of God, Jesus fed them. It is clear from this response that for Jesus the way out was always the way *through*. To him, the solution to the problem could not be found through running or hiding, but through facing it squarely; facing it head-on; facing it directly and courageously; facing it with trust in God.

That's the first thing we find here—Jesus chose to cope rather than run. Now here is a second key to coping with life's problems.

Second, Jesus Trusted God and Used the Available Resources

Jesus surveyed what resources were available, and he used them to solve the problem. Sometimes we fail to do this. The problem looms so large and seems so formidable that we suffer from tunnel vision, from narrow vision, from closed-mindedness, and as a result we are blinded to the available resources, the available tools, and the available opportunities. We don't even see them.

A few weeks ago, I watched Robert Redford's film *The Natural*, in which he plays a brilliant baseball player. (One man commented that this is the perfect movie for him and his wife: *he* loves baseball and *she* loves Robert Redford!) In *The Natural*, Robert Redford portrays an outstanding baseball player named Roy Hobbs, who is a naturally gifted athlete. At the age of nineteen, he is on his way to try out with the Chicago Cubs when he meets with misfortune and mysteriously disappears. Then, some fifteen years later, around the age of thirty-four, he shows up to play baseball for a fictional Major League team called the New York Knights. Roy Hobbs walks into the dugout with a five-hundred-dollar contract in his hand and reports to the manager, a crusty old baseball character named Pop.

The manager, Pop, thinks it's a joke. The Knights' players laugh and snicker at this thirty-four-year-old rookie named Roy Hobbs. A thirty-four-year-old rookie! This is unheard of. Rookies are nineteen, twenty, twenty-one—not thirty-four. Thirty-four is when many retire from baseball, not when they start. Pop tries to get rid of him, but Roy Hobbs won't leave. He has a contract. So they give him a uniform and put him on the bench.

Day after day, the New York Knights baseball team plays terribly. They get worse and worse. They can't hit, they can't field, and they can't score; they drop lower and lower in the standings. Then it's revealed that the manager, Pop, is in an awful predicament. He has a tremendous problem. In addition to being the manager, Pop is also one of the owners. Because the team is playing so poorly attendance has fallen off, and the Knights are in a dire financial situation. Pop has had to borrow money from a mobster and now he is in big trouble. His only hope is to win the pennant. If the New York Knights don't finish the season in first place, Pop will lose everything—his team, his job, his investment, and his place in baseball. Here Pop is, in this terrible situation. He is frustrated, worried, and scared; and he doesn't realize it, but he has the greatest baseball player who ever lived sitting on the bench. Finally, they give Roy Hobbs a chance. They let him take batting practice. They throw him five pitches. He hits all five out of the park! Pop sees this available resource, and he puts Roy Hobbs in the lineup. Hobbs, with his great play, inspires the other players and they begin to win. And they keep on winning, and they win the pennant. (The movie has a happy ending. I love happy endings!)

The point is that Pop made the mistake we often make. He didn't realize the available resource he had right there under his nose in the dugout. We get so blinded by the enormity or complexity of our problems that we don't see or use the resources we have right at our fingertips.

Some years ago, in a small Mississippi Delta town, a man was driving a little foreign car when the back right wheel came off. When the wheel came off, it broke all four of the lug bolts that attach the wheel to the car. The man had a big problem. There were no lug bolts that he could buy in that small town. The closest parts store was twenty miles away. What in the world could he do? The police, the fire department, the mayor, and even the men playing checkers on the courtyard square gathered around, but no one could figure out what to do.

Then along came Crazy Leroy, as he was known. He was the town character. The townspeople called him Crazy Leroy because he sometimes did bizarre things and because he often didn't appear to be very bright. The men decided to tease Crazy Leroy, so they brought him over; showed him the car, the wheel, and the broken lug bolts; and asked him what he would do if it were his car. "Very simple," said Leroy. "The other three wheels have four lug bolts. I would take one off each wheel and use those three to attach this wheel, and then I would drive to Jackson and buy four new lug bolts." The crowd was amazed and they cheered for Leroy, and then they asked him how he figured that out. Leroy replied, "I may be a little crazy, but I'm not stupid."

It's amazing what you can do if you just use the available resources. Jesus found out quickly that the crowd had five loaves and two fish. He took what they had and used it to the best of his ability, and he trusted God—and God made it enough. God took the little and made it much. God took the little and made it work. God took the little and made it enough.

When we trust God and use what we have the best we can, God takes our little and makes it much. Jesus chose to cope rather than run, and he used the available resources.

Third and Finally, Jesus Turned the Problem into an Opportunity

Jesus turned what looked like a defeat into a victory. He turned a burden into a blessing. We can do that too.

There is an old legend of how birds got their wings. According to the legend, the little birds didn't have wings at first, so they would just scamper about on the ground. But one day God got worried about them. So that night, while the birds were asleep, God attached wings to their sides.

The next morning when the little birds woke up they felt so burdened and bothered by those heavy, cumbersome things attached to their sides. They felt so awkward and weighted down, and it was such a problem for them to move about. Those wings were such a nuisance. They complained and fussed and felt sorry for themselves. But then some of the birds began to move the wings, and they were surprised at how graceful it felt. They exercised their wings, and then suddenly some of them began to fly. Then others began to try it, and *they* flew also.

Now, the point of the legend is obvious, a beautiful lesson for life, namely this: what seemed at first to be a heavy, great burden to the little birds became their means of flight, the means by which they could soar into the skies.

You see, our problems can become opportunities. Our problems can become the means by which we soar into a higher level of living, a higher level of maturity, and a higher level of faith. With the help of God, with God on our side, we can cope; and so we know that we can live triumphantly now.

CHAPTER EIGHT

You Can't Take It with You, So Live Serenely Now

The Grace of Serenity

SCRIPTURE: MATTHEW 27:11-14

One of the most impressive emblems of Holy Week is the serenity of Jesus in those difficult hours and days that led to the cross. His strength of character is nothing short of amazing—his deep sense of peace; his quiet confidence; his inner calm; his courage; his serenity of spirit; whatever you want to call it. We see it vividly, especially in that scene where Jesus is on trial before Pontius Pilate. Look at Jesus. He stands there poised, confident, unafraid, and serene. He is facing death, but his strength never wavers.

Just think of it:

- an unfair trial for an innocent man;
- lies, plotting, conniving;
- bribed witnesses, political intrigue;
- jealousy, hostility, hatred;
- a mob scene and a "kangaroo court."

And in the face of it all, Jesus displays an incredible quality of inner peace and strength and calm. They betray him, deny him, taunt him, beat him, curse him, spit upon him, and nail him to a cross, and he says, "Father, forgive them; for they do not know what they are doing." Now, that is strength of character, isn't it? That is inner peace. That is serenity.

Real serenity comes not from outer circumstances or having many possessions or worldly power. It comes from inner stability, and in that respect, Jesus was the most serene man who ever lived. He was the embodiment of what we now call the Serenity Prayer.

In the summer of 1934, the famous theologian Reinhold Niebuhr was vacationing at his summer cottage in Heath, Massachusetts. He was invited to conduct a worship service at a small church nearby. At the end of the service, Dr. Niebuhr offered this prayer: "God, give us the grace to accept with serenity the things that cannot be changed, courage to change the things which should be changed, and the wisdom to distinguish the one from the other." After the service, a neighbor came up and said he had been particularly touched by the prayer and wondered if he could get a copy of it. Dr. Niebuhr reached into his Bible, took out a crumpled sheet of paper, and said, "Here, take the prayer. I have no further use for it."

The next Christmas, that neighbor used the prayer on his Christmas cards, and the founder of Alcoholics Anonymous saw it and adopted it as the official prayer for A.A. Then the U.S.O. picked it up and reprinted millions of copies of the prayer for servicemen during World War II.

Today it can be found everywhere—on greeting cards, plaques, and banners—all over the world. I'm sure that the man who originally wrote the prayer had no idea that millions of people across the face of the earth would one day find help and inspiration through this little prayer offering of only thirty-four words. The Serenity Prayer, as we now affectionately call it, may well be the best-known prayer of the twentieth century.

God, give us the grace to accept with serenity the things that cannot be changed, courage to change the things which should be changed, and the wisdom to distinguish the one from the other.

Now, what is it about this prayer that makes it so special to so many? I think it is because the prayer deals with three basic realities, namely, (1) that life has limits that we must accept, (2) that life has great possibilities for us if we have the courage to tackle them, and (3) that it takes wisdom to tell these apart.

Let's take a look at each of these phrases in the prayer one at a time in the hope that we may learn a little more about what serenity is and how it was such an important part of the mind and personality of Jesus.

God Gives Us the Grace to Accept with Serenity the Things That Cannot Be Changed

There are some things that cannot be changed. There are certain "givens" that we have to learn to live with that will not budge and cannot be altered. No matter how much work or energy we give to the process, it is just a fact that there are some things in life that will not be changed. Life has limits. Life has heartaches. Life has disadvantages. The Christian answer is the serenity of acceptance, even the redemption of our handicaps.

Back in 1951, the Peabody Award for Entertainment in television was given to a comedian known and loved all over the world. His name was Jimmy Durante. That same year Gene Fowler published the story of Durante's life. Born in 1893 in one of the poorer homes in New York City, Jimmy Durante had an unusual countenance—a huge nose that he and others might have considered a serious limitation. But Jimmy Durante learned how to live with his limits. He not only accepted his nose, but he used it and made it one of his greatest assets, and with his unique facial feature he won a special place in the hearts of the world. His comment about it has become a classic: "Everybody's got a schnozzola!" That's the serenity of acceptance.

All of us know the impact Helen Keller had on this world. What serenity she possessed as she powerfully responded to great limitations and challenges, and rose above them with strength and grace.

Remember William Barclay. His daughter and her fiancé were killed in a tragic boating accident just a short time before they were to be married. It was hard to accept. Barclay wrote:

> When things like that happen, there are just three things to be said. First, to understand them is impossible. Second, Jesus does not offer us simple solutions to them. What he does offer us is his strength and help somehow to accept what we cannot understand. Third, the one fatal reaction is the bitter resentment which forever after meets life with a chip on the shoulder and a grudge against God. The one saving reaction is simply to go on living, to go on working, and to find in the presence of Jesus Christ the strength and courage to

meet life with steady eyes. (William Barclay, *Testament of Faith* [London: Mowbrays, 1977], 45-46.)

There are some things we just can't change. Serenity comes from recognizing that and going on with life, doing the best we can and knowing that God is with us, and knowing that we can trust God to bring it out right.

Second, God Gives Us the Courage to Change the Things Which Should Be Changed

We tend to fear and resist change, so *courage* is indeed the key word here. A vital part of the good news of our faith is that change is possible. We can be changed. Ernest Fitzgerald, in his book *How to Be a Successful Failure*, tells a fascinating story about a young man who was caught stealing sheep. The young man was charged and convicted. As a penalty, the villagers decided to brand his forehead with the letters ST, meaning, of course, "Sheep Thief."

The brand was a constant source of shame for the young man. Penitent, he asked God for forgiveness to help him overcome his problem. With courage, he had determination not to be remembered as a thief. He began to live in a new way, giving to others in every way. He performed endless small acts of kindness for everyone. He was kind, thoughtful, helpful, compassionate, and always dependable.

Years and years went by. One day a visitor came to the village. The visitor saw the man and wondered about the letters on the man's forehead. He asked the people of the village what the letters ST stood for. Strangely, no one could remember, but they suspected that ST was an abbreviation for the word *saint*.

Change can happen, but it takes courage.

In the sixteenth century there lived a brilliant man named Martin Baal. Martin Baal concluded after much research and agonizing prayer that there were certain things wrong in the church of his time. He listed them and seemed to understand that most of them were a result of a loss of the biblical doctrine of justification by faith. Martin Baal folded his paper on which his conclusions were written and then hid them behind the stones in the wall of his monastery room.

There was another Martin who lived at the same time and who reached the same conclusions. His name was Martin Luther, but Luther didn't hide his ideas. He had the courage of his convictions. He nailed his "Ninety-five Theses" on the most public place he could think of, the door of Castle Church in Wittenberg, Germany, and the Protestant Reformation began.

Two men named Martin. Both saw the need for change, but history reserves a place only for the one who had the courage to act.

Here again is where we see the greatness of Jesus. He was the conscience of society. He saw things happening that were wrong. People were being hurt, mistreated, and exploited, and he had the courage to act. "God, give us the grace to accept with serenity the things that cannot be changed, [but give us the] courage to change the things which should be changed."

Third, God Gives Us the Wisdom to Distinguish the One from the Other

Life has limits and life has great possibilities, but how do you know which is which? How do you know which to tackle?

A private in the army was assigned to KP (kitchen patrol). He was given the duty of sorting potatoes into three barrels marked "large," "medium," and "small." A few hours later, the sergeant found the private a nervous wreck, beside himself, tearing out his hair, muttering under his breath, with virtually none of the work done. When the sergeant asked what was going on, the private replied, "These decisions are killing me!"

Decision making is hard. It takes wisdom to do it right. But how does wisdom come? Not quickly, not suddenly; there is no instant wisdom. It has to be grown, cultivated, sharpened, and developed over a long period of time.

The psalmist knew this, and that is why he said, "So teach us to number our days / that we may get a heart of wisdom" (Psalm 90:12 ESV). What does that mean? It means that every day is a new learning opportunity, a new chance to discover more about God and God's truth, God's world, and God's will for our lives.

It's interesting that the word for "wisdom" in Hebrew is *Shama.* It means "believing obedience," believing something so much that you stake your life on it, and it comes only from spending time with God—a lot of time with God in prayer; a lot of time in Sunday school and church; a lot of time in the study of the Scriptures.

One day a young administrative assistant, in conversation with her boss, expressed a value judgment. The man said to her, "Where did you get that idea? From that funny little church you go to?" At first, the boss's harsh question bothered the young woman, but then she regained her composure and replied, "I'm glad my 'funny little church' shows."

Let me ask you something: When you go out into the

world today and tomorrow and the next day, will your "funny little church" show? Will your faith show? Will the Spirit of Christ show? Will the wisdom that comes only from spending time with God show? This is what the Apostle Paul meant when he spoke of "the mind of Christ." Have within you "the mind of Christ." Spend so much time with Christ that his mind becomes yours. Spend so much time with Christ that you begin to think and act like him. There is no greater wisdom than that, and no greater serenity.

CHAPTER NINE

You Can't Take It with You, So Live Patiently Now

"The Impatient Itch for the Instantaneous"

SCRIPTURE: MARK 15:21-32

Norman Cousins, in his book *The Healing Heart*, tells of an unforgettable experience he had some years ago in the Los Angeles airport. (This was before cell phones.) He was between flights and needed to make a quick telephone call to his office. He put a quarter (the only change he had in his pocket) into the phone, but somehow something went wrong and he didn't get a dial tone. He pressed the coin-return button, but to no avail. Nothing happened. His quarter did not come back! Frustrated, with no more available change and with no time to go get any, he began to jiggle the phone's hang-up lever until finally an operator came on the line. He explained to her what had happened, how he had lost his only quarter, and he asked the operator if she would please push the button to send his money back so he could try again.

"I'm sorry, sir," she said, "I can't do that, but if you will give me your name and address, the phone company will be glad to mail it to you."

"Come on, now, Operator!" Cousins said. "Please, just push the button and send me my quarter. That would be so much simpler."

"I'm sorry, sir. Give me your name and address, and we will be glad to mail it to you."

"But, I need it now!"

"I'm sorry, sir. Give me your name and address, and we will be glad to mail it to you," repeated the operator.

"You mean to say that you are going to send me a check for a quarter in the mail using an envelope and a twenty-two-cent stamp? [That's what stamps cost back then!] That's ridiculous! Couldn't you just..."

"I'm sorry, sir," intoned the operator, "Give me your name and address, and we will be glad to mail it to you."

At this point, Cousins decided to try the coin-return button one more time. You won't believe what happened: it was like the jackpot with a Las Vegas slot machine. Quarters literally began pouring out of that telephone, quarters and dimes and nickels pouring out faster than he could catch them, in magnificent and overflowing profusion. There were quarters pouring out and spilling onto the floor.

"Operator, Operator, are you still there?" asked Cousins. Then he said, "Operator, something quite remarkable has just happened. All I did was press the coin-return button and the machine is giving me all its earnings. Quarters are pouring out and the flow hasn't stopped yet."

"Sir," the operator said, "will you please put the money back in the box?"

Now, let me ask you something: What would *you* have said in that situation? Well, Norman Cousins said it: "Operator, I'm very sorry. I can't do that, but if you will give me your name and address, I'll be glad to mail it to you!"

Isn't that a wonderful story? It shows us that things can come back to haunt us. It also dramatically shows how we love instant results. If anything is characteristic of the times in which we live, it is, as J. Wallace Hamilton called it, the "impatient itch for the instantaneous." We want everything in a hurry these days: instant coffee, instant oatmeal, one-hour cleaning, pay one dollar down, and get it now.

We are *impatient people*, looking for near ways and quick results, so much so that God's patient ways sometimes confuse and perplex us. We are in a hurry, while "God's mills grind slow but sure." We look for the quickest route, but God refuses to take shortcuts. And sometimes, because of our impatient ways, God's long-suffering patience frustrates us and we begin to point a finger at God and shout out demands and issue ultimatums. "Now, listen here, God," we say. "We want some answers and we want them now! Give us some fast explanations! Give us some instant answers! Give us a dramatic sign and be quick about it!"

Just think about it for a moment: there is a dramatic contrast between our modern ways of thinking and acting, our "impatient itch for the instantaneous," and God's patient ways. We are impatient; but God is deliberate, steady, and long-suffering. We look for the speedy way, the shortcut, the instant answer, the immediate solution; but God takes the long way around. God refuses to be rushed. And sometimes in our fast-paced, hurried, harried world we find it hard to understand the slow-but-sure ways in which God works. Let's think about this together for just a few moments.

Look First at How Patient God Is

Over and over, we see it in the Scriptures. The writers of the Bible were convinced that one of the crowning attributes of God is God's long-suffering patience, God's steady, infinite patience.

Remember the Exodus. God led the people of Israel out of Egyptian slavery to the Promised Land; but notice God led them the long way around. It was only two hundred miles from Egypt to Canaan—ten days' journey by camel caravan back then. Today, it would be less than an hour by airplane, or close to three hours by car. Think about it—only two hundred miles from the place of slavery to the land of promise, but it took the people of Israel forty years to get there, the long way, the way of patience.

Maybe there is a sermon here for us in our spiritual pilgrimage. God led them not by the near way, but by the long way around. So short a way to go—two hundred miles; so long a time to get there—forty years. Why? The New Testament says it was because of their unbelief (see Hebrews 4:6), which is just another way of saying that they were not ready for it. The way of the wilderness was for them "the way of preparation." They were not really prepared for the Promised Land. It took time to get them ready. It took time to mold them into a people and make them into a nation. There in the wilderness they received the Ten Commandments and became God's people. It was their "getting ready time."

You see, the point is clear: promised lands can't be entered too quickly.

"Too much, too soon" is the perfect formula for frustration, heartache, and mediocrity. When we *get* too easily and *reach* too quickly, we tend to appreciate too lightly. Promised lands have to be prepared for, worked for, longed for, waited for, and deeply wanted. I would venture to guess that many of our disappointments come from grasping too eagerly for good fruit that isn't yet ripe. We like the shortcut, but God takes the long way around—the way of slow, deliberate maturing, the way of long-suffering patience.

Also, *remember the temptation experiences of Jesus in the wilderness at the beginning of his ministry* (see Matthew 4:1-11; Mark 1:12-13; Luke 4:1-13). The enticement to take shortcuts was precisely what the temptations were all about. Jesus was tempted to take shortcuts in bringing the Kingdom. He was tempted to use the petulant way of power, the expedient way of political strategy, the ruthless way of military might, and the crowd-pleasing way of magic; but he refused to give in to any of these and chose instead the slow, deliberate way of love, the patient way of the Suffering Servant, and the painful way of the cross.

Remember the Crucifixion scene—Jesus hanging there on a wooden cross. The people mock and taunt him: "If you are the Christ, show us, give us a sign, come down from the cross right now, and then we will believe." Even as you read it, you feel yourself wishing that he would. You almost wish God would show them, but again God refuses to make the power play; God refuses to take the shortcut. God chooses instead the long way around. Again, we see it; God chooses the way of love and persuasion and patience. How patient is our God. But let's look at the other side of that coin.

Look Next at How Impatient We Are

It's one of the key differences between God's way and ours. We're in a hurry; God isn't. We want instant solutions, but God brings us along slowly. We are petulant; God is patient. We like the shortcut, the direct route; God works mostly by indirection. God takes the long way around, and this is sometimes hard for us to understand. Most of us can relate to that little one-sentence prayer: "God, give me patience, and give it to me right now!"

Martin Luther couldn't understand how God could continue to put up with us. "If I were God," he said, "and the world treated me as it had treated Him, I would kick the wretched thing to pieces." And I suppose Luther might have. But not so with God. God is patient, forgiving, and long-suffering.

J. Wallace Hamilton graphically described this contrast between God and us. He wrote:

> Go out in the woods and remember how God makes a tree. Sit by a great rock and remember how God fashioned the world. It didn't happen in a moment, as a magician waves his hand.... One of the most characteristic words of the Bible is the word "wait."... "Wait on the Lord."... The whole idea (of waiting) of course runs counter to the modern temper.... Who wants to wait for anything today? We're an aggressive generation, impatient with delays or detours, or even disciplines. We want things done at once. The push button has become our symbol.... "Why wait?" "Pay one dollar

down," "Get it now," "Clothes cleaned—one hour," "Cars washed—two minutes." The itch for the instantaneous... instant biscuits, instant coffee, instant cereal.... We are impatient people, looking for near ways, shortcuts, quick results. (J. Wallace Hamilton, *Serendipity* [Westwood, NJ: Revell, 1965], 157-58.)

I saw a cartoon recently that pictured a little boy shopping with his parents in a supermarket. The boy picked up a box of something and brought it to the shopping cart. "Oh no, Son," said his parents, "put it back. You have to *cook* that!" Oh, how impatient we are! But, it's not that way with God. God takes the long, deliberate, steady-but-sure way, the way of patience and love. Maybe it's because God knows in God's great wisdom a very special truth.

And that brings us to point three.

The Things That Matter Most Take Time

God's patient ways are right because the things that really matter take time to cultivate. To be sure, some things you can get immediately by pushing buttons or rubbing something on, or by paying something down— you can have them now. Some things you can acquire by the direct route and the shortcut, and I don't mean to minimize that. But the great things, the real values, do not come that way. They have to be grown and cultivated and developed. You can get a sports car or a big-screen television with a quick down payment. But character, maturity, morality, and spiritual strength are things you have to wait for, work at, want desperately, and grow, slowly but surely.

There is a delightful children's anthem written by

Natalie Sleeth entitled "Little by Little," which has this key line: "Good things that are here to stay, / don't get done in just one day."

Retired professional basketball player Larry Bird, who played for the Boston Celtics, is without question one of the greatest basketball players in NBA history. He won the Most Valuable Player Award in the National Basketball Association three years in a row. How did he become so great? Well, Larry Bird was legendary for his amazing dedication to the game of basketball. He worked at it. He practiced constantly. One opposing player told of arriving at the Boston Garden arena with his teammates to play the Celtics. It was several hours before an important game, and there was the great Larry Bird, standing at the free-throw line of the dark, deserted Boston Garden, practicing free throws over and over again. The coach of the opposing team preached a little sermon to his team about hard work and dedication to the game, using Larry Bird as the prime example. He said, "I heard some of you fellas on the plane talking about Larry Bird and how nice it would be to be a natural-born superstar. Well, let me tell you, there are no natural-born superstars. Larry Bird is a superstar because he works at it, and that's what it takes—a lot of discipline, a lot of dedication, a lot of sacrifice, a lot of practice, a lot of hard work."

Some weeks later, that same team returned to Boston to play the Celtics again. This time they arrived a day early and went immediately to the Boston Garden to practice. The Garden was cold and empty. Larry Bird was not at the free-throw line. "OK, Coach," chided one of the players, "where is Larry Bird?" The other players chimed in, teasing their coach, "Yeah, Coach, where is he? Where's the superdedicated, hardworking Larry Bird?" The coach smiled good-naturedly. But then one of the players said, "Wait a minute. I think I hear something." Everyone got really quiet. They heard a noise above them. They looked up and saw a solitary figure, running laps like a rookie, on the catwalk in the top of Boston Garden. It was Larry Bird!

It's true in sports, in music, in business, in education, in family life, in personal maturity: the things that matter most don't come overnight; they don't come instantly; they have to be grown, cultivated, and developed over a long period of time, with a lot of hard work.

It's also true *spiritually*. How do you develop a meaningful prayer life? It doesn't come suddenly. You have to work at it. You have to practice and practice and practice some more. How do you become a good student of the Scriptures? It doesn't come suddenly. There is no easy way to master the Bible. You have to spend time with it. You have to work at it. You have to read, study, discuss, and reflect. You have to turn to the Bible commentaries and the Bible dictionaries, and then go back and read and study some more. It takes time, discipline, and hard work. How do you become a great churchperson? Well, as Bishop Hazen G. Werner put it some years ago, there are "no saints suddenly." It takes practice, commitment, and dedication. Get in the church; get involved; come every time the doors are opened. Love it, serve it, cherish it, and share it with others. Center your life on the church. Work at it. Give it time. How do you become a spiritually mature person? Well, it takes time. We don't leap from babyhood to adulthood in a moment. It takes time and a lot of experience to become a mature person. God wisely made life. God ordered it in specific stages, and if we skip a stage or two, we are headed for trouble.

A young woman came to my office some time ago in deep trouble. One of her relatives said, "Her trouble is that she got too much too soon. She grew up too fast. She was thrust into a situation she just wasn't prepared for or ready to handle." It takes time and experience to become a mature person. The way to become a spiritually mature Christian is to spend so much time with Christ that we begin to think and act like him; to spend so much time with him that we take on what Paul called "the mind of Christ." It just takes time and effort and commitment.

There are no easy, magical, instant solutions. There are no overnight spiritual superstars. So, we had just as well forget that. What we need to remember is that the things that matter most take time, effort, commitment, discipline, a lot of practice, a lot of hard work, and a lot of patience. So, with God's help, live patiently now.

CHAPTER TEN

You Can't Take It with You, So Live Purposefully Now

The Power of a Purpose

SCRIPTURE: MATTHEW 6:25-33

One evening, some years ago, I was feeling terrible. My head was throbbing. My stomach was in knots. I was physically worn out and completely exhausted. I prescribed for myself a nap on the couch in the den. My head had just hit the pillow when the phone rang. A voice on the line gave me the bad news that one of our most devoted church members (and a good friend) had just died. His wife was still at the hospital; she needed help. Could I go?

I was up and going out of the door in less than five minutes, and guess what? As I drove toward the hospital, I made an amazing discovery. Suddenly my headache was gone, and the internal queasiness I had felt only moments before had completely subsided. I didn't feel tired or weak anymore. I felt a deep sadness over the loss of a friend. I felt compassion for his wife and family who had so suddenly been thrust into a state of shock and into the valley of grief. But in my concern to help, and in my intense desire to be a friend and a pastor, I had been forced by the situation to get outside myself. As a result, all of my ailments, which had seemed so severe and so taxing just brief minutes earlier, literally had gone away!

Isn't that incredible? Some people would call that "instant recovery"; others might call it a "second wind"; and still others would call it "overcoming self-pity." But I would call it "the power of a purpose." For, you see, a sense of purpose gives us power to do things we never dreamed possible!

For example, I once read a story about a woman who pulled a two-thousand-pound car off her little boy after they had plunged into a ditch. "He was pinned under the car," she said, "and I didn't even think about how heavy the car was. I just knew I had to get it off him, so I did!" Some people would call that "hysterical strength" or "adrenalin might," but I would call it "the power of a purpose."

Two women entered the hospital on the same day and had the same operation. It took one of them a full year to recuperate, and all through the year she complained about how much she was suffering. The other woman was up and going strong, working and taking care of household tasks within ten days. Why? What was the difference? The difference is found in the fact that the woman who got well so quickly *had* to: she had three preschool children at home to care for. Once again, we see it—the power of a purpose!

It's so important to have a purpose. We see this underscored boldly in the grand old story of Nehemiah's rebuilding of the broken walls of Jerusalem. It seemed such a hopeless task with the walls in ruins, the people scattered, and everyone so discouraged and despondent. And all around were enemies who wanted no strong Jerusalem and who did everything in their power to prevent it from becoming strong. They tried ridiculing Nehemiah first, and then they tried persuasion. They scoffed; they taunted; they criticized; they threatened. But Nehemiah went right on with his work as though he didn't know they were there. Four times the demand went up and four times the answer came back from Nehemiah: "I am doing a great work and I cannot come down" (Nehemiah 1:1–6:3).

Isn't it refreshing to find in this Old Testament passage a man so committed to a purpose that nothing could discourage him; no criticism could distract him; no side issue could pull him away! The power of a purpose: "I'm doing a great work and I cannot come down."

Nehemiah's single-minded commitment reminds me of the story about a man who met a bulldog on a narrow path one day. The bulldog never slowed down, never hesitated, and never veered to the right or to the left. The bulldog just kept on walking with eyes straight forward until the man had to jump out of the way and let him pass. As the bulldog walked by, the man said a simple prayer: "O Lord, give me just a little bit of what that bulldog has a whole lot of!"

Purpose, commitment, single-mindedness, dedication to a great cause—whatever you want to call it—gives meaning to life. It's the fiber of Christianity.

But what is our purpose? Jesus helps us here. In fact, that is why he came: to show us the purpose of life; to show us what God wants us to do and be.

He put it something like this in the Sermon on the Mount: "The purpose of life is to seek first the kingdom of God and God's righteousness, and everything then falls in place for you. Dedicate your life to serving God and then trust God to bring it all out right" (see Matthew 6:33).

On another occasion, Jesus said something along the lines of: "Your real purpose in life is to love God and to love people. Just do that, commit your life to doing that, and your life will be full and rich and zestful and meaningful because you will be in harmony with God's purpose, and that purpose will give you power for the living of these days."

Look at some of the ways purpose can give us power.

Purpose Gives Us Power to See Problems as Opportunities

We see this dramatically in Nehemiah. He saw a run-down Jerusalem not just as a problem, but also as an opportunity for him to do something great for his people and for God. Nehemiah easily could have given up, thrown up his hands, and said, "It's no use. Jerusalem is done for. Israel has had it." But no; rather, he said, "I will rebuild the city." You see, if you know your purpose, it gives you the "eyes of faith" to see problems as opportunities.

Remember the story about the two shoe salesmen who were sent to a remote part of the world to open up a new market. Three days after their arrival, the first salesman sent a cablegram that read: "Returning home on next plane. Can't possibly sell shoes here. Everybody goes barefoot."

Nothing was heard from the second salesman for about two weeks. Then came a fat airmail envelope with this message for the home office: "Fifty orders enclosed. Many more to come. Prospects unlimited. Great opportunity. Nobody here has shoes." Purpose gives us the power to see problems as opportunities.

Purpose Gives Us the Power to Rise above the Fear of Criticism

Any time we do something responsible, any time we give leadership, any time we take a stand, we open ourselves to criticism. Nehemiah came back to Jerusalem and began to rebuild the walls of that great ancient city. As he worked, his enemies taunted him, made fun of him, whispered behind his back, ridiculed him, and laughed at him; they criticized him mercilessly. But Nehemiah kept right on working, and he answered, "I'm doing a great work and I cannot come down."

During the American Civil War, Abraham Lincoln was criticized slanderously, scathingly, but he was committed to saving the Union. He had a great purpose, and he said, "If I were to try to read, much less answer, all the attacks made on me, this shop might as well be closed for any other business. I do the very best I know how—the very best I can; and I mean to keep doing so until the end.... If the end brings me out wrong, ten angels swearing I was right would make no difference" (Henry J. Raymond, *The Life and Public Services of Abraham Lincoln* [New York: Derby & Miller, 1865], 753). Lincoln was committed to a great purpose, and that gave him the power to rise above the fear of criticism.

Like Nehemiah before him, Lincoln was saying, "You can criticize me if you must, but I am doing a great work and I cannot come down."

Purpose Gives Us the Power to Make Decisions

How are you at decision making? Some people have a terrible time making any kind of decision because they have not really made that essential, ultimate decision about the purpose of life.

Have you heard the story about the man who seemed unable to commit himself to anything? Once when he was trying to order breakfast in a restaurant the waitress suggested eggs and then asked how he liked his eggs. He answered, "I like them fine, thank you."

"No, no," the waitress said, "I mean, how do you like them *cooked*?"

The man replied, "I like them *that* way best of all!"

Decision making is indeed a problem for many people. However, if we have made our ultimate decision then other decisions fall more easily into place. For those of us who call ourselves Christians, Christ is the measuring stick for all our decisions. When we face big decisions it helps to ask questions such as:

• What is the most loving, Christlike thing to do in this situation?
• Can I do this and still be faithful to Christ?
• Can I do this and put God first at the same time?
• What can I do in this situation to express love for God and God's children?

You see, if we know our purpose, that gives us the power to make good decisions.

Purpose Gives Us the Power to Live Meaningfully

When we have a sense of purpose, it makes us happy, productive, and whole. Our lives become zestful, creative, and meaningful. I am convinced that what people want and need more than anything else is meaning in their lives—a sense of mission; a great dream; an urgent cause; a commitment that really matters; a destination. Remember that fascinating slice of dialogue in *Alice's Adventures in Wonderland.* Alice, speaking to the Cheshire Cat, asked:

"Would you tell me, please, which way I ought to go from here?"
"That depends a good deal on where you want to get to," said the Cat.
"I don't much care where—" said Alice.
"Then it doesn't matter which way you go," said the Cat.
"—so long as I get *somewhere*," Alice added as an explanation.
"Oh, you're sure to do that," said the cat, "if you only walk long enough."
(Lewis Carroll, *Alice's Adventures in Wonderland* [New York: Macmillan, 1898], 89-90.)

Many people drift through life with no sense of direction and miss their meaning. They never find their purpose, and they come up empty-handed, frustrated, depressed, and ashamed. When one famous writer came to the end of her life, she said that she was ashamed of all her stories and plays—all of them. She said not one of them would she dare show to God.

The purpose of life, according to Jesus, is to seek

God's kingdom, to love God, and to love people. Anything less is not worth much. If you know your purpose, it makes life meaningful and zestful and joyous.

Purpose Gives Us the Power to See the Routine, Mundane, and Commonplace as Sacred

Remember Jesus' appreciation of little things; brooms, candles, water, leaven, old cloth, birds, seeds, sunsets, wind, and the flowers of the fields were holy to Jesus. They were sacred to him because they spoke to him of the Father.

I ran across an old "Peanuts" cartoon that makes the point. Charlie Brown, Linus, and Lucy are lying on their backs on a hillside, looking at the clouds. Lucy says, "If you use your imagination, you can see lots of things in the cloud formations. What do you think you see, Linus?"

Linus answers, "Well, those clouds up there look to me like the map of British Honduras on the Caribbean. That cloud up there looks a little like the profile of Thomas Eakins, the famous painter and sculptor. And that group of clouds over there gives me the impression of the stoning of Stephen. I can see the Apostle Paul standing there to one side."

"Uh huh," said Lucy, "that's very good. What do *you* see in the clouds, Charlie Brown?"

"Well," answered Charlie Brown, "I was going to say I saw a ducky and a horsie, but I changed my mind!"

We can all relate to Charlie Brown, can't we? But when we find our impossible dream, our unique mission, our special cause, our real purpose, then everything speaks to us of God. We become "sermonic bloodhounds," sniffing out God's truth everywhere.

Everywhere we look, everything we see reminds us of God and all that God has lovingly prepared for us. Every bush becomes a "burning bush," calling us, as Moses was called, to go to work for God. Every place becomes a sacred place to celebrate God's love and presence. If we know our purpose, it gives us power—power to see problems as opportunities, power to rise above criticism, power to make good decisions, power to live life meaningfully, and power to see the sacred, even in mundane, commonplace things. So, the call is loud and clear: live purposefully now.

CHAPTER ELEVEN

You Can't Take It with You, So Live Uniquely Now

Celebrating Your Uniqueness

SCRIPTURE: 1 CORINTHIANS 12:4-11

S ome years ago, a woman had a pet parakeet named Chippy. The woman was cleaning Chippy's cage with a canister vacuum cleaner one morning, while Chippy watched from his perch. When the phone rang, the woman reached for the receiver while continuing to vacuum the cage. This was not a good idea, for just as the woman picked up the phone she heard the horrible squawking noise of Chippy the parakeet being sucked into the vacuum cleaner. In panic, the woman ripped open the bag and emptied its contents. Chippy fell out among the fluff—a bit stunned, and very dirty, but still alive. Now, if all this weren't traumatic enough, the woman then grabbed Chippy, ran out into the kitchen, and thoroughly doused him under the water faucet.

Later, an enterprising reporter went to cover the story. After the reporter heard the unfortunate tale, he asked the woman, "Tell me, how is Chippy doing?" The woman replied, "Well, Chippy really isn't so chipper these days. He doesn't sing much anymore. He just sits and stares!"

That story is something of a parable for what happens to many people in our world today. They get knocked around by the troubles of the world and thoroughly doused with the stresses and problems of our time, and they lose their spirit and just blend into the woodwork. Like Chippy, they don't "sing" much anymore; they just sit and stare.

How tragic it is when we stop singing our song. How sad it is when we quit on life, because each of us has a special and unique part to play in the tapestry of God's handiwork. It is so important to see this: every person has a special part to play. Every person is a unique child of God. We must not miss this. We dare not take that uniqueness away. The loving human being understands that, sees that, embraces that, and celebrates that.

The Bible speaks of our uniqueness as a special gift from God. Some folk are apostles; some are prophets; some are teachers. The body of Christ does not consist of one member, but many, and all are needful; all are helpful (see 1 Corinthians 12:14-26). God must have loved variety; God made so much of it.

As individuals, we must not be satisfied with just becoming like everybody else, with just quitting on life and blending into the woodwork, with just sitting and staring. Also, on the other side of the coin, we must avoid the temptation to force our way upon everybody else. You see, each of us is special in the mind of God. Each of us is unique in the plan of God. We are different and that is wonderful. Some are tall and some are short. Some like Beethoven and some like Carrie Underwood. Some love opera and some love football. We have different temperaments, different interests, different opinions, and different gifts—and that's OK. Indeed, it is beautiful as long as we are loving about it, as long as we are kind about it, and as long as we are tolerant and understanding about it.

But here is the rub: if we are insecure, then we tend to see everyone who is different from us as a threat to us. Then, when that happens, we become scared and panicky, and we react by trying to force our way upon them. We want to make other people be like us. We want to make them do it *our* way. We feel compelled to prove that "my way is the right way," the valid way, the only way. And we may think those other people over there who see it differently are cruel or stupid or insensitive. So then we choose up sides. That is precisely what had happened in the Corinthian church, and that is why Paul had to write to them to straighten them out.

When Paul wrote to the Christians in Corinth, they were in big trouble. Their church was torn apart by their differences. They had chosen sides and split into factions. There was misunderstanding and there was suspicion. There was blatant immorality. There were lawsuits among the church members. There were arguments, accusations, and infighting. There were struggles for power and position. Their differences were killing them spiritually. So Paul wrote to them, and, in essence, he said, "It's OK to be different."

Your uniqueness is God's gift to you, and the loving person is the one who sees that and embraces that. If only we could learn how to disagree without being disagreeable. If only we could learn to celebrate our own uniqueness and the uniqueness of others. The key to doing that is love.

Look at how Paul develops that in 1 Corinthians. In the first eleven chapters, he exposes the people's sins and outlines their problems.

Then, in chapter 12, he shows them that it's OK to be different. Some have *this* gift and some have *that* gift. Some have *this* talent and some have *another* talent. Some can do *this* and some can do *that*. We are different, but God made us that way. God made each of us to be unique, and God can blend our differences and use them for good. So stop squabbling over who is right and who is wrong. Stop quarreling over whose way is best. Paul says he wants to show them a better way, a more excellent way, the best way of all. And with that, Paul bursts forth with his classic "love chapter," 1 Corinthians 13:

> What does it matter if you can speak in the tongues of men and angels? If you are not loving, you are only so much noise, like an irritating gong or a clanging cymbal. What does it matter if you are brilliant? What does it matter if you have miraculous faith? What does it matter if you can do impressive, mind-boggling things? If you are not loving, it is not worth anything.
>
> Love is patient and kind. Love is not jealous or boastful. Love is not arrogant or rude. Love does not insist on its own way. Love is not irritable or resentful.
>
> All these other things will pass. Only love will last forever, so make love your aim, put love first. How important it is that we learn how to love. (author's paraphrase)

There is a disturbing line in the play *Mame* that reads like this: "Life is a banquet and most poor [people] are starving to death." The people who are starving are those who have never learned how to love.

One of our most respected educators in America once said that he is concerned about our educational system because "we are teaching our children the 3 R's but failing to teach our children how to love" (Leo Buscaglia, *Living, Loving & Learning*, ed. Steven Short [New York: Fawcett Columbine, 1983], 5). We are stuffing them with facts and forgetting that they are people.

Now, with this all in mind let me raise a question: Who is the loving person? What is he or she really like? How would you describe the loving human being? Here are a few ideas to try on for size.

First, the Loving Person Celebrates His or Her Own Uniqueness

Remember the opening words in the book *Born to Win*:

Each human being is born as something new, something that never existed before. Each is born with the capacity to win at life. Each person has a unique way of seeing, hearing, touching, tasting, and thinking. Each has his or her own unique potentials—capabilities and limitations. Each can be a significant, thinking, aware, and creative being—a productive person, a winner.

The words "winner" and "loser" have many meanings. When we refer to a person as a winner, we do not mean one who makes someone else lose. To us, a winner is one who responds authentically by being credible, trustworthy, responsive, and genuine, both as an individual and as a member of society. A loser is one who fails to respond authentically. Martin Buber makes this distinction as he retells the old story of the rabbi who, on his deathbed, is asked if he is ready for the world to come. The rabbi says yes. After all, he will not be asked, "Why were you not Moses?" He will only be asked, "Why were you not yourself?" (Muriel James and Dorothy Jongeward, *Born to Win* [Reading, MA: Addison-Wesley, 1996], 1.)

You see, our personality is our uniqueness. To be a loving person, I need to first discover who I am, what is unique about me, and then seize that, embrace that, develop that, and celebrate that. I must not be content to become like everybody else. I must have the courage to do my own thing and to be the best person I can be. Only then can I reach out to others with love. Only then can I give myself to others. Only then can I be a loving person.

Strange as it may sound, this is sometimes difficult to do because more often than not the system tries to make us be like everybody else. There's an old story about an animal school, a wonderful story that educators have used for years. In this story, some animals decided to start a school. They met to write a curriculum.

The rabbit wanted a course on running.

The bird wanted a course on flying.

The fish wanted a course on swimming.

The squirrel wanted a course on tree climbing.

So they put all the courses in and they required all the animals to take them. The rabbit was magnificent in running but failed flying, swimming, and tree climbing. The bird did beautifully in flying but had trouble with running and swimming. The squirrel led the school in tree climbing but flopped miserably in all the other courses. And when graduation time came, the valedictorian was a "slow-thinking" eel who could do a little of all of it. (And as a result the owl dropped out and now votes no on all tax elections that have to do with schools!)

As individuals we must work at making our own unique contribution. We dare not be satisfied with just becoming like everybody else.

Some years ago, Hal Luccock said something that relates to this. He said that in detective stories when a crime is committed and no fingerprints are left, they call it a perfect crime. Then Hal Luccock, in his special way, would say that it is also a crime, indeed, when we don't leave our fingerprints anywhere. How sad it would be to live a lifetime and leave no trace that we had been here. How sad to leave no fingerprints.

To be a loving person you don't have to be John Wesley or Saint Francis or Mother Teresa or Moses. All you have to be is the best you can be.

There is a wonderful story about Oliver Wendell Holmes going out for a walk one evening some years ago. As he was walking along, a little girl came up and asked if she could walk along with him. "Well, of course," said the distinguished jurist, "I'd be happy for you to." So the two of them walked along the road together and enjoyed each other's company.

As the shadows began to lengthen and it started to get dark, the little girl said that she had better start back toward home. As she turned to leave, her famous companion said, "Now if you get back home and your mother asks where you have been, just tell her that you've been walking with Oliver Wendell Holmes." And the little girl said in reply, "I will. And when *you* get home and *your* folks wonder where *you've* been, just tell them that you've been walking with Mary Susanna Brown!"

I like that story because it reminds us of something very important, namely this: in God's world, Oliver Wendell Holmes was a very special person, and so was Mary Susanna Brown, and so are you.

That's the first thing to underscore: the loving person celebrates his or her own uniqueness. Now, here is a second thought.

Second, the Loving Person Celebrates the Uniqueness of Others

This means that we must give other people the same freedom to be unique, to be different from us. We must give them the freedom to disagree with us, and we must still be big enough to accept them, to value them, and to love them.

Have you heard about the man who found the neighborhood children playing in his freshly poured and still soft and wet concrete drive? He came unglued and gave the children a tongue-lashing that would have made a sailor blush. The man's wife came out of the house and said, "George, I'm surprised at you. I thought you *loved* children." "I do," answered George, "but I love them in the *abstract* and not in the *concrete!*"

But you see, it is not enough to love others abstractly. We have to love them concretely, personally, and specifically. Do you realize what that means? It means that we must avoid labels. We must beware of simplistic stereotyping. We must beware of ignorant name-calling. We must beware of labels that insult or arouse suspicion and create mistrust. With labels, we teach fear and hatred; we teach prejudice and bigotry; and we therefore miss the integrity and the uniqueness of the person. Labels can be so hurtful and so detrimental. We hear the label and think we know everything about that person. But no one bothers to ask, Does this person cry? Does he feel? Does she understand? Does she have hopes and dreams? Does he love his kids?

Labels: avoid them like the plague. If you are a loving person, you will not only celebrate your uniqueness, but you will also be big enough to celebrate the uniqueness of others.

That brings us to a third idea.

The Loving Person Celebrates the Uniqueness of Life as a Partnership with God

There is a joke that has been making the rounds in recent years, and it makes an interesting theological point. A man is trapped in his house during a flood. When the water comes up to his front porch, a boat comes to take him to safety. "No," the man says, "I will stay here. I have faith in God. God will save me."

When the floodwaters get to the second floor of the house, a second boat comes to get the man. "No," he says, "I will stay here. I have faith in God. God will save me."

Later, the water is still rising, and the man is straddling the roof when a helicopter arrives for him. "No," the man says, "I will stay here. I have faith in God. God will save me."

Next, we see the man entering the gates of heaven. He has drowned in the flood. Immediately, he demands an audience with God and exclaims, "Lord, I had faith that you would save me from the flood!" And God replies, "Look, I sent two boats and a helicopter. What did you expect?"

Life is partnership with God, and we have to do our part. You see, I don't know of anything that will make us more loving than seeing ourselves as God's partners. When we see ourselves as God's partners, then we see all people as God's beloved children, and we love them, respect them, and value them as God's family, as our brothers and sisters. Also, when we see life as partnership with God, then God's will and God's cause become foremost in our minds. We stop worrying about our rights; we stop trying to get our way; we put God's way at the forefront; and we become more loving. The camp song "Spirit of the Living God" sums it up beautifully: "Spirit of the living God...melt me, mold me, fill me, use me." And to add to that: spirit of the living God, help me celebrate my uniqueness and help me celebrate the uniqueness of others. Help me live uniquely now.

CHAPTER TWELVE

And Trust God for Tomorrow

"Do It Again, Lord; Do It Again"

SCRIPTURE: ACTS 2:37-42

The great preacher and writer Dr. Leslie Weatherhead once told a wonderful story about his visit some years ago to the place where John Wesley, the founder of Methodism, had his famous heartwarming Aldersgate experience. Unfortunately, the little Aldersgate chapel doesn't exist anymore. It's been long since torn down. Now there is just a plaque on the side of a building that marks the spot. But at the time of Leslie Weatherhead's visit, there was a chapel.

Weatherhead described that experience like this. He said that on the side of one of the pews in the dimly lit chapel there was a small plaque with a tiny light over it. The plaque read, "On this spot on May 24, 1738, John Wesley's heart was strangely warmed." Being in that special place was a moving moment for Weatherhead, and he wanted to bask in the glow of it for a while. So he walked to the back of the chapel and sat down on the last pew to think and pray and reflect.

Suddenly the door of the chapel opened and in came an older man wearing a heavy, tattered overcoat and walking with the help of a cane. The older man, not seeing Weatherhead in the darkness of the chapel, slowly walked down the center aisle. When he got alongside the John Wesley pew, he noticed the plaque. Curious, he walked over to the plaque, bent down, and read the words out loud: "On this spot on May 24, 1738, John Wesley's heart was strangely warmed." Immediately, the older man dropped down on his knees, looked upward, and said, "Do it again, Lord. Do it again for me." Isn't that a wonderful story? And isn't that a great prayer? "Do it again, Lord. Do it again for me. Warm my heart."

We are not exactly sure what happened to John Wesley at Aldersgate some 250 years ago. We certainly couldn't begin to put it into words. That kind of experience defies description. Words aren't adequate to express or capture a spiritual moment like that. But we do know this: the heartwarming experience gave John Wesley a new life, a new warmth, a new energy, a new purpose, and a new power. And it produced a new church. Somehow, the fire of the Holy Spirit brushed across his heart and set John Wesley aflame.

Did you know that during his ministry John Wesley rode more than twenty-five thousand miles on horseback? That's a quarter of a million miles, a distance roughly equal to ten complete trips around the globe. On a horse!

Did you know that he preached more than forty

thousand sermons and that he and his brother Charles wrote close to seven thousand hymns?

Did you know that John Wesley developed many cures for diseases, wrote a book on medicine, and started clinics for the poor?

Did you know that John Wesley said that churches should be built in the octagonal form and that the interior should have a rail in the middle to divide the men from the women? (Now, Mr. Wesley said many brilliant things; *that* was probably not one of them!)

Did you know that at John Wesley's death in 1791, his followers numbered seventy-nine thousand in England and forty thousand in America, but by 1957 there were forty million Methodists worldwide? Did you know that today there are approximately seventy-five million Methodists? (For these and other facts and statistics about John Wesley see "John Wesley: Did You Know?" in *Christian History & Biography*, Issue 2 [January 1, 1983].)

Did you know that for all the power of his eyes, his voice, and his witness for Christ, John Wesley was only 5 feet, 3 inches tall and weighed 128 pounds? This man, small of physical stature, became a spiritual giant. Why? Because his heart was strangely warmed; because he received the gift of the Holy Spirit.

That is precisely what happened to the disciples of Jesus at Pentecost. Remember that they were powerless before the Holy Spirit came; but when they received the gift of the Holy Spirit, it warmed their hearts, it set them aflame, and they turned the world upside down.

Justin Wroe Nixon put it like this: "The basic difference between physical power and spiritual power is that we use physical power, but spiritual power uses us"

(Wilson O. Weldon, *Mark the Road* [Nashville: Upper Room,1973], 85).

We see it dramatically in the experiences of Simon Peter. Relying upon his own strength, he failed miserably. Over and over, he said the wrong things at the wrong time. In a panic, he tried the way of the sword. And then in crunch time, he denied his Lord three times. But then, when the Holy Spirit exploded into his life, Simon Peter got fired up; he did the best he could and trusted God to bring it out right. And when he preached that day at Pentecost, three thousand souls were saved (see Acts 2:37-42).

We also see it graphically in the experiences of John Wesley. Relying on his own strength, he went to the then new American colony of Georgia as a missionary, and failed miserably. But then at Aldersgate Wesley's heart was strangely warmed. He realized that God was with him. He trusted God and did the best he could, and incredible, miraculous things happened.

The writer of Acts was on target when he called the Holy Spirit a "gift." It is indeed a gift from God that can turn our lives around; that can take our feeble efforts and use them in amazing ways; that can turn our weakness into strength and our defeats into victories. Let me show you what I mean.

First, the Holy Spirit Redeems Situations

The Holy Spirit can take a bad scene and convert it, and use it for good. This truth is powerfully portrayed in a true experience that happened to Zan Holmes. Dr. Holmes is one of the great and distinguished preachers in the United States, and he tells of something that happened to him when he was a first-year seminary student. His church was so proud of him and his call to the ministry. His pastor, Dr. I. B. Loud, asked him to read the scripture, and then Zan settled back to listen to the sermon. But Dr. Loud did something very unusual that morning. He stepped into the pulpit and mentioned how proud everybody was of Zan Holmes and his efforts to become a minister. And then Dr. Loud surprisingly announced that he thought it would be a good idea if "Brother Zan would come to the pulpit and deliver the sermon of the morning!"

Dr. Holmes said he nearly died right on the spot! He was terrified as he walked from his chair to the pulpit. He thinks there are still fingernail marks gouged into the wood of the pulpit where he clutched it for dear life as he tried to think of something—anything—to say.

Finally, he remembered a sermon that he had been working on for preaching class. His mind raced, and he began to preach that sermon. He said it was pretty good, all three-and-a-half minutes of it, but then he ran out of steam. He felt so alone, so empty, so vulnerable, so defeated as he stood before that anticipating congregation. It was an awful moment. He couldn't think of anything to say. And then, Zan Holmes began to cry. But then he heard the voice of an older woman in the congregation say, "Help him, Lord Jesus." Then came the familiar voice of a man from the bass section of the choir. It boomed out, "Come, Holy Spirit."

Holmes then looked down on the front pew and saw two precious little girls who suddenly began to clap their hands in rhythm and sing that familiar spiritual "Amen." Before long, the entire congregation was clapping and singing, and Holmes said, "I just stood there and watched God work." Zan Holmes said he learned a valuable lesson that morning: "It is the Holy Spirit who finishes the sermon."

If we do the best we can, God will do the rest. That's what happened at Pentecost. Simon Peter did his best and let God finish it. He did his best and then stood back and watched God work. God does not ask us to be successful; God only asks us to be faithful. If we give our all, if we do our best, if we genuinely try to do God's will, then God will bring it out right. The Spirit of God can take a weak voice and make it a trumpet. The Spirit can take a defeat and turn it into a victory. The Holy Spirit can redeem situations.

Now, here is a second thought.

Second, the Holy Spirit Reminds Us of the Truth

Throughout the Scriptures, the Holy Spirit is "the truth giver." The Holy Spirit comes to reveal God's truth.

Dr. Fred Craddock is one of the great teachers of preaching in our country. He tells a moving story about something that happened to him in the early days of his ministry. He was helping with Vacation Bible School. He said, "It used to last for two weeks, but there were so many 'casualties' among the teachers that we reduced it to one week!"

Dr. Craddock said that he had this group of young children who were driving him up the wall, especially after ten days with them, and especially one boy in the class. Craddock described that difficult boy like this: "There was this one boy in the class who . . . well, let me put it like this. Have you ever had somebody in class that was so bad that you were glad when they were absent? He was that type! And, quite honestly, I had written him off. 'He's not paying attention,' I thought. 'He doesn't care. He doesn't want to be here. He is not interested in the lessons. He is only interested in seeing how crazy he can drive me and in disrupting the class. He is hopeless.'"

Dr. Craddock said he had gotten so worn out with it all that he was now simply trying to think of things for the students to do to keep them busy and out of his hair. He thought of something: he decided to send them outside on a study of creation. He gathered them at the door and said, "Now listen. When I ring the bell, I want you all to scatter and go outside and find one of God's miracles, and then when I ring it again, come back and show us what you have and tell what it teaches us about God."

Craddock rang the bell, and the students scattered. He said that his plan was not to ring it again. But, he did. After a while he rang the bell and the students came back with God's miracles.

"Well, what do you have?" Dr. Craddock asked. One little boy had a rock. The boy said, "This rock reminds us that God is stout and God made the world." One little girl had a flower. She said, "Only God could make a flower like this. It's so pretty!" Another little girl had a leaf that had fallen off the tree and had turned brown. She said, "God made the seasons of the year—summer, fall, winter, spring." Another boy stepped forward with some huckleberries. He said, "God provides for us. He feeds the animals and he feeds us!"

"Well, that's great," said Dr. Craddock, and then he looked over and saw that "not-so-nice" boy standing off to one side with nothing in his hands. He was standing there, holding the hand of his little sister, who had been in her kindergarten classroom. Craddock thought, "What is he doing? Why won't he cooperate? I guess they are going to leave early. Why didn't somebody tell me?"

Then, this conversation took place.

"Leaving early?" Dr. Craddock asked the boy.

"No, sir."

"Well, did you bring anything?"

"Yes, sir."

"What did you bring?"

"My little sister."

"Your little sister?"

"Yes, sir."

"Why did you do that?"

"'Cause she's God's miracle. I prayed for a little sister, and God gave me one. She's the best miracle I know of!"

Fred Craddock said that he stood there stunned because he knew the little boy was right, and he knew that God was there in that room, in that moment, closer than breathing. Craddock said, "I don't know what ever happened to that boy, but I hope he's still doing that. He was the only one in the class—including the teacher—who got the point."

The Holy Spirit touched that little boy's heart when no one was looking and gave him the truth—the truth that God's greatest miracles are people! "You want to see one of God's miracles? I'll go get my sister!"

This is one of the greatest truths of the Bible. We (you and I) are made in the image of God. Talk about a miracle! God made the squirrels, the elephants, the giraffes, and the duck-billed platypuses; God made the trees, the flowers, and the skies. God made all of it and said, "That's good! Now, *that's good!*" And to cap it all off, God said, "Now for the masterpiece. I'm going to create something like myself." And God made you. And it is a sin for us to say, "Well, I'm only human."

If you want to see one of God's miracles, don't gather the pinecones; don't capture the squirrel; don't find a picture of a trout stream. Just look at the person seated next to you; look at the people you find in your life. *There* is God's miracle. There is the crown of God's creation. Sometimes when we least expect it, the Holy Spirit reveals the truth. That's what happened in that Vacation Bible School classroom that morning.

There's another lesson here, namely this: don't ever write anybody off. And, whatever you do, don't write off the Holy Spirit. That's what Pentecost teaches us: the Holy Spirit redeems situations. The Holy Spirit reminds us of the truth.

Third and Finally, the Holy Spirit Restores Our Strength

Simon Peter was down, defeated, and embarrassed. He had failed; he had denied his Master at the critical moment. He had seen the Crucifixion and was devastated. He had met the resurrected Christ, but still he felt like a failure. He felt inadequate for the task. But then came the Holy Spirit, and Simon Peter's strength was replenished. Empowered by the Spirit he became a man of courage, a tower of strength. The Holy Spirit restores our strength.

Some members of our church were going through a difficult valley some time ago. It was one of the toughest situations you can imagine. I went to try to minister to them, and they ministered to me. They said, "Don't worry about us now. We are going to make it. We are taking this one day at a time, and God is with us as never before. God is giving us strength. God will see us through."

That is the "good news" of our faith, isn't it? God never deserts us. God redeems situations for us. God reminds us of the truth and restores our strength.

Now, let me conclude with this story once told by politician Adlai Stevenson. A young man approached his girlfriend's father to ask for permission to marry the man's daughter. The father was skeptical. He said, "You don't know what you are asking. She has very extravagant tastes. I doubt very much that you will ever be able to support my daughter. I'm a wealthy man and I can barely manage it myself." The young man thought for a moment and then said, "Sir, I believe I have it. You and I could just pool our resources!"

Now, that's the message of the Christian faith, isn't it? We are not alone. God is with us. We can pool our resources with God, and God's strength will see us through. God's strength will carry us; God's strength will save us in this life and in the world to come. And so the lesson is this: with God's help, and by God's grace, and with the strength of God's Holy Spirit, do your best now. And trust God for tomorrow.

DISCUSSION GUIDE

Suggestions for Leading a Study of James W. Moore's
Have You Ever Seen a Hearse Pulling a Trailer?

John D. Schroeder

This book by James W. Moore explores the truth that we can't take the material possessions we've accumulated with us when we die, so instead of putting our faith in material things, we should put our faith in God and focus on the things in life that money can't buy.

To assist you in facilitating a discussion group, this study guide was created to help make this experience beneficial for both you and members of your group. Here are some thoughts on how you can help your group:

1. Distribute the book to participants before your first meeting and request that they come having read the first chapter. You may want to limit the size of your group to increase participation.

2. Begin your sessions on time. Your participants will appreciate your promptness. You may wish to begin your first session with introductions and a brief get-acquainted time. Start each session by reading aloud the snapshot summary of the chapter for the day.

3. Select discussion questions and activities in advance. Note that the first question is a general question designed to get discussion going. The last question is designed to summarize the discussion. Feel free to change the order of the listed questions and to create your own questions. Allow a set amount of time for the questions and activities.

4. Remind participants that all questions are valid as part of the learning process. Encourage their participation in discussion by saying there are no "wrong" answers and that all input will be appreciated. Invite participants to share their thoughts, personal stories, and ideas as their comfort level allows.

5. Some questions may be more difficult to answer than others. If you ask a question and no one responds, begin the discussion by venturing an answer yourself. Then ask for comments and other answers. Remember that some questions may have multiple answers.

6. Ask the question "Why?" or "Why do you believe that?" to help continue a discussion and give it greater depth.

7. Give everyone a chance to talk. Keep the conversation moving. Occasionally you may want to direct a question to a specific person who has been

quiet. "Do you have anything to add?" is a good follow-up question to ask another person. If the topic of conversation gets off track, move ahead by asking the next question in your study guide.

8. Before moving from questions to activities, ask group members if they have any questions that have not been answered. Remember that as a leader, you do not have to know all the answers. Some answers may come from group members. Other answers may even need a bit of research. Your job is to keep the discussion moving and to encourage participation.

9. Review the activity in advance. Feel free to modify it or to create your own activity. Encourage participants to try the "At home" activity.

10. Following the conclusion of the activity, close with a brief prayer, praying either the printed prayer from the study guide or a prayer of your own. If your group desires, pause for individual prayer petitions.

11. Be grateful and supportive. Thank group members for their ideas and participation.

12. You are not expected to be a "perfect" leader. Just do the best you can by focusing on the participants and the lesson. God will help you lead this group.

13. Enjoy your time together!

Suggestions for Participants

1. What you will receive from this study will be in direct proportion to your involvement. Be an active participant!

2. Please make it a point to attend all sessions and to arrive on time so that you can receive the greatest benefit.
3. Read the chapter and review the study-guide questions prior to the meeting. You may want to jot down questions you have from the reading, and also answers to some of the study-guide questions.
4. Be supportive and appreciative of your group leader as well as the other members of your group. You are on a journey together.
5. Your participation is encouraged. Feel free to share your thoughts about the material being discussed.
6. Pray for your group and your leader.

Chapter 1

You Can't Take It with You, So Live Confidently Now: "Have You Ever Seen a Hearse Pulling a Trailer?"

Snapshot Summary

This chapter encourages confident living through placing our confidence in the promise of God, the truth of Christ, and the strength of the Holy Spirit.

Reflection / Discussion Questions

1. What is the meaning of the saying, "You can't take it with you when you go"? What truth is there in that saying?
2. Tell what it means to be confident, and give an example of confidence.
3. Where does confidence come from? How do you gain confidence?

4. According to the author, in what sorts of things does the world want us to place our confidence? Would you agree with the author on this point? Why or why not?
5. What are some of the best things in life that money can't buy?
6. Talk about why we can put our confidence in the promise of God. How are we blessed when we do this?
7. Reflect on / discuss some of the reasons people don't put their confidence in God.
8. What does it mean to be confident in the truth of Christ?
9. What do we need to do in order to put our confidence in the strength of the Holy Spirit?
10. What additional thoughts or ideas from this chapter would you like to explore?

Activities

As a group: Give one another a vote of confidence by sharing affirmations and encouragement with one another. These can be written down or expressed verbally. Or locate verses in the Bible that can serve as sources of confidence, and share why the verses you selected are meaningful.

At home: Take steps this week to increase your confidence through meditation, serving others, self affirmations, and talking to God.

Prayer: *Dear God, thank you for reminding us that we can live confidently now because of your love and care for us. Help us encourage confidence in others and live a life of confidence that is pleasing to you. Amen.*

Chapter 2

You Can't Take It with You, So Live Faithfully Now: A Faith for Ordinary Times

Snapshot Summary

This chapter looks at faithful living by examining issues related to discipleship, including its challenges, commitments, and costs.

Reflection / Discussion Questions

1. Share what it means to you to live a faithful life.
2. Do you think it is tougher to have faith in easy times or difficult times? Explain your answer.
3. What does the writer of Hebrews say about faith?
4. How does having a strong faith help with ordinary, day-to-day frustrations?
5. Recall an early time in your life when you felt God touched you, something that inspired you to take that initial leap of faith. Describe that experience.
6. What does the author mean by "the original challenge of discipleship"?
7. Why is it easier to make commitments than to keep them?
8. What types of faith commitments do we make as Christians?
9. What does it mean to say that "discipleship costs"? What are some of the costs of discipleship?
10. What additional thoughts or ideas from this chapter would you like to explore?

Activities

As a group: Let each group member create a short message of faith that could appear on a car bumper sticker. Share your creations.

At home: Conduct a self-assessment of your faith, and be intentional in how you express your faith this week.

Prayer: *Dear God, thank you for giving us all that we need in order to live a faithful life. Forgive us when we fall short. Help us to be faithful to you in word and deed. Amen.*

Chapter 3

You Can't Take It with You, So Live Peacefully Now: The Most Godlike Thing in the World

Snapshot Summary

This chapter reminds us that peacemakers are patient, loving, Christlike people.

Reflection / Discussion Questions

1. Name some times and situations in life when a peacemaker is needed.
2. Reflect on / discuss what it means to serve as a peacemaker.
3. Why is the quality of patience so highly valued?
4. Why does it help to have patience when acting as a peacemaker?
5. Name some famous peacemakers, living or dead. What special qualities have enabled these persons to be influential in spreading peace?
6. Why do love and peace go together?

7. Explain what is meant by saying that peacemakers are Christlike people.
8. What are some ways in which everyone can be a peacemaker?
9. What did Jesus teach us about patience, love, and peace?
10. What additional thoughts or ideas from this chapter would you like to explore?

Activities

As a group: Create a "peace treaty" for all nations and people of the world. Ask each member to contribute a universal right or principle of peace to add to your document. Or experience five minutes of peace through a quiet time of meditation and prayer, ending with a group prayer.

At home: Look for opportunities this week to serve as a peacemaker.

Prayer: *Dear God, thank you for the peace you give us that no one can take away. Help us serve as your peacemakers and live peacefully in this world. Amen.*

Chapter 4

You Can't Take It with You, So Live Victoriously Now: Beating Depression

Snapshot Summary

This chapter looks at some of the causes of depression and offers a few suggestions for dealing with it.

Reflection / Discussion Questions

1. What are some of the common symptoms of depression?
2. Reflect on / discuss some of the causes of depression as outlined by the author.
3. According to the author, why is it important to remember that depression is temporary?
4. How can laughter and talking to others help relieve depression?
5. What are some of the spiritual tools Christians have available to fight depression?
6. How do people satisfy and recover from spiritual hunger?
7. What is meant by the statement, "Love and work conquer everything"?
8. Brainstorm ways you can help someone who is suffering from depression.
9. What does it mean to "live victoriously now"?
10. What additional thoughts or ideas from this chapter would you like to explore?

Activities

As a group: Let each group member locate a Bible verse that provides hope and healing in difficult times. Share why the verses you selected are meaningful.

At home: Consider your own spiritual hunger. What simple things can you do to help satisfy your hunger for God?

Prayer: *Dear God, thank you for reminding us that we can deal with depression through your help and your love. Help us remember those who are suffering and offer others our love and encouragement to be healthy, victorious Christians. Amen.*

Chapter 5

You Can't Take It with You, So Live Boldly Now: Use It or Lose It

Snapshot Summary

This chapter is about using our talents—or risk losing them—in the physical, intellectual, social, and spiritual levels of life.

Reflection / Discussion Questions

1. Reread the parable of the talents (Matthew 25:14-29). Why is this parable misunderstood? What does it mean?
2. Give an example of a talent that could be lost if it is not used.
3. Why are exercise and practice so important for maintaining physical talents?
4. Name some ways you can stretch your mind to enhance intellectual talents.
5. Name different types of social interaction that improve social talents and skills.
6. Reflect on / discuss how spiritual growth is born, and how it dies.
7. What risks and sacrifices are associated with using your talents?
8. What often prevents people from living boldly?
9. Name a person whom you feel lived or lives boldly.
10. What additional thoughts or ideas from this chapter would you like to explore?

Activities

As a group: Create a list of acts of extraordinary boldness that ordinary people could use to help an individual or a group in need.

At home: Conduct an inventory of your talents, and assess whether they are being used. Put one of your talents to use this week to help someone.

Prayer: *Dear God, thank you for all of the talents and skills we have been given. Help us use them wisely. Open our eyes to opportunities to share our talents with others. Amen.*

Chapter 6

You Can't Take It with You, So Live Courageously Now: Rising above Disillusionment and Disappointment

Snapshot Summary

This chapter encourages conquering disappointment by loving others, encouraging others, and worshiping with others.

Reflection / Discussion Questions

1. Share a time when you felt disappointed or downhearted.
2. What are some of the causes of disillusionment?
3. According to the author, what symptoms of disillusionment were shown by Cleopas and Simon on the Emmaus road?
4. Why is loving other people a key to overcoming disillusionment?

5. Describe some of the many benefits of loving others.
6. Give examples of some words of encouragement that bring healing.
7. How does worshiping with others help us live courageously?
8. How can God help us deal with all of life's disappointments?
9. Name some of the keys to courageous living.
10. What additional thoughts or ideas from this chapter would you like to explore?

Activities

As a group: Use your Bibles to locate acts of courage by early believers. Talk about the examples you have chosen and how they speak to you on a personal level.

At home: Look for an opportunity this week to help a downhearted person.

Prayer: *Dear God, thank you for lifting us up when we are down. Help us live courageous lives inspired by your love. Remind us that we have nothing to fear. Amen.*

Chapter 7

You Can't Take It with You, So Live Triumphantly Now: You Can Cope

Snapshot Summary

This chapter shows how to cope with problems by following the example of Jesus, who chose to cope rather than run, who trusted God and used available resources, and who turned problems into opportunities.

Reflection / Discussion Questions
1. Share a time when you attempted to outrun a problem.
2. Reflect on / discuss why people use and abuse drugs.
3. Why are drugs not the answer?
4. What lessons can we learn from Jesus' feeding the five thousand in the wilderness?
5. Give some reasons why people run rather than cope.
6. Name some of the many resources and organizations available today that can help people deal with problems.
7. As your comfort level allows, share a difficult time in your life when you trusted God and did your best with the resources at hand.
8, Explain how problems can become opportunities. Give an example.
9. What does God want us to do with our problems?
10. What additional thoughts or ideas from this chapter would you like to explore?

Activities

As a group: Let each person write down a problem in the form of a prayer request. Collect the requests for use in a group prayer. Distribute the requests to members of the group so that each member has a person and a request to pray for this week. Or create paper bookmarks for your Bibles by writing down a verse that reminds you that through God, you can cope with any problem.

At home: Talk with God about the problems with which you are dealing. In prayer, turn your problems over to God.

Prayer: *Dear God, thank you for turning our problems in life into opportunities. Remind us of all the resources we possess to cope with any challenge that comes our way. Amen.*

Chapter 8

You Can't Take It with You, So Live Serenely Now: The Grace of Serenity

Snapshot Summary

This chapter shows that we can live serenely because God gives us serenity, courage, and wisdom to face any challenge.

Reflection / Discussion Questions

1. How would you define serenity? Give an example of it.
2. Reflect on / discuss how Jesus demonstrated serenity when facing death.
3. What do you think makes the Serenity Prayer so special to so many people?
4. Name some things in life that can't be changed, where serenity would be required.
5. Share a time when God gave you serenity during a difficult time of life.
6. Why do people often fear and resist change?
7. Where does courage come from? When is courage needed?
8. How do you know when change is possible?
9. Where does wisdom come from? Name some sources of wisdom.
10. What additional thoughts or ideas from this chapter would you like to explore?

Activities

As a group: Let each group member write down the Serenity Prayer on a piece of paper to serve as a reminder and a resource, at work and at home. On each paper, draw a symbol that represents serenity. Share your creations.

At home: Examine yourself and your life to identify an area in which you need courage to change. Take a small step this week toward making that change.

Prayer: *Dear God, thank you for giving us the serenity, courage, and wisdom to face any challenge. Remind us that you are with us in difficult times. Grant us faith to trust in your deliverance. Amen.*

Chapter 9

You Can't Take It with You, So Live Patiently Now: "The Impatient Itch for the Instantaneous"

Snapshot Summary
This chapter reminds us of the patience of God, how impatient we are, and how the things that matter most take time.

Reflection / Discussion Questions
   1. Share a time when you were either patient or impatient about something.
   2. What causes us to be impatient?

3. Where does patience come from? How is it developed?
4. Reflect on / discuss the patience of God and give some examples of it.
5. Compare and contrast the patience of God with the patience of humans.
6. Name some of the things that matter most and which take time.
7. Describe the work and patience needed to develop a meaningful prayer life.
8. When you need to be patient, what should you do?
9. What new insight about patience have you gained recently?
10. What additional thoughts or ideas from this chapter would you like to explore?

Activities

As a group: Create your own brief prayers that you can use when patience is needed. Write down your prayers, and share them. Or explore the question, "What does patience look like?" Use your creativity to draw a portrait of patience.

At home: Practice patience all week, and note the difference it makes in your life.

Prayer: *Dear God, thank you for being patient with us. Remind us to be just as patient with ourselves and with others. Amen.*

Chapter 10

You Can't Take It with You, So Live Purposefully Now: The Power of a Purpose

Snapshot Summary
This chapter shows the benefits of living a purposeful life.

Reflection / Discussion Questions
1. Share a time when you experienced the power of having a purpose.
2. Name some of the benefits of having a purpose.
3. What lessons can we learn about purpose from Nehemiah's rebuilding of the walls of Jerusalem?
4. Reflect on / discuss the author's comment that purpose is "the fiber of Christianity."
5. How does Jesus help us know our purpose?
6. Name some problems that could also be seen as opportunities.
7. How does purpose help us rise above the fear of criticism?
8. Reflect on / discuss the connection between having a purpose in life and decision-making.
9. What new insight about the power of purpose did you gain from this chapter?
10. What additional thoughts or ideas from this chapter would you like to explore?

Activities

As a group: Write down some of the purposes you have in life—for example, goals to achieve, people to help, or your calling from God. Share your statements of purpose.

At home: Reflect upon your own purpose and your journey toward achieving that purpose.

Prayer: *Dear God, thank you for the chance to live a life filled with opportunity and purpose. Help us rise above the fear of criticism and base our decisions and actions on the fulfillment of your ministry. Amen.*

Chapter 11

You Can't Take It With You, So Live Uniquely Now: Celebrating Your Uniqueness

Snapshot Summary

This chapter shows how to celebrate your own uniqueness, the uniqueness of others, and the uniqueness of your life as a partner with God.

Reflection / Discussion Questions

1. Share something unique about yourself.
2. Name some ways to celebrate your uniqueness.
3. What circumstances or problems can, at times, take our uniqueness away?
4. Explain the importance of tolerance and appreciating the differences in others.
5. Reflect on / discuss what Paul had to say about uniqueness and gifts.
6. Name some keys to being a loving person.
7. Describe some ways to celebrate and encourage uniqueness in others.
8. What is the connection between uniqueness and our partnership with God?
9. Who encouraged your uniqueness as a child or as an adult? How have they helped you?

10. What additional thoughts or ideas from this chapter would you like to explore?

Activities

As a group: Create unique symbols as reminders of your own uniqueness. Share your creations.

At home: This week, celebrate your own uniqueness and the uniqueness of others.

Prayer: *Dear God, thank you for making each of us unique and different. Help us use our unique skills and abilities to minister to others. Amen.*

Chapter 12

And Trust God for Tomorrow: "Do It Again, Lord; Do It Again"

Snapshot Summary

This chapter is about trust and how the Holy Spirit redeems situations, reminds us of the truth, and restores our strength.

Reflection / Discussion Questions

1. Share a time when you trusted in God for tomorrow.
2. What impresses you about the life and faith of John Wesley?
3. Reflect on / discuss how the Holy Spirit changed the life of the disciples.
4. How does the Holy Spirit redeem situations? What do we need to do in order for this to occur?

5. Share a time when you felt the strong presence of the Spirit of God in your life.
6. Name some of the ways the Holy Spirit reminds us of the truth. Why is this important?
7. What does it mean to say that we are one of God's miracles? Why is this significant?
8. Name some times when we need the Holy Spirit to restore our strength.
9. Describe some different ways we can trust in God for tomorrow.
10. What additional thoughts or ideas from this chapter would you like to explore?

Activities

As a group: Celebrate the successful conclusion of this study with a graduation party. You may want to include food, create diplomas, and provide a time for sharing.

At home: Reflect upon your reading and discussion of this book. What have you learned? How has it made you a better Christian? What further changes would you like to make in your life?

Prayer: *Dear God, thank you that we can trust in you for all our tomorrows. Remind us that the Holy Spirit is always ready to assist us in living a fruitful life. Amen.*